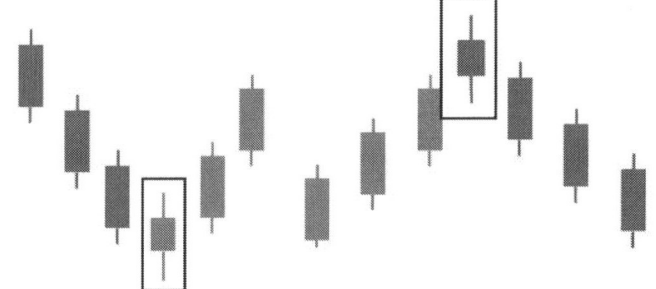

THE CANDLESTICK TRADING BIBLE

INVENTED BY MUNEHISA HOMMA

The most successful trader in history

THE CANDLESTICK TRADING BIBLE

Content

Introduction	4
Overview	6
History of Candlesticks	8
What is a Candlestick	11
Candlestick Patterns	14
The Engulfing Bar Candlestick	16
The Doji Candlestick Pattern	20
The Dragon Fly Doji Pattern	22
The Gravestone Doji Pattern	25
The Morning Star	28
The Evening Star Candlestick Pattern	31
The Hammer Candlestick Pattern	34
The Shooting Star Candlestick Pattern	37
The Harami Pattern	40
The Tweezers Tops and Bottoms	43
Candlestick Patterns Exercise	47
The Market Structure	51
How to Trade Trending Markets	54
Support and Resistance Levels	58
How to Draw Trendlines	61
The Ranging Market	63
Time Frames and Top Down Analysis	70
Trading Strategies and Tactics	79
The Pin Bar Candlestick Pattern Strategies	81

Trading the Pin Bar Candle With The Trend	*88*
Trading Tactics	**92**
Trading Pin Bars with Confluence	*96*
Pin Bar Trades Examples	*100*
Trading Pin Bars in Range Bounds Markets	*103*
The Engulfing Bar Candlestick Pattern	**109**
How to Trade the Engulfing Bar Price Action Signal	*112*
Trading the Engulfing Bar with Moving Averages	*117*
How to Trade the Engulfing Bar with Fibonacci Retracements	*120*
Trading the Engulfing Bar with Trendlines	*122*
Trading the Engulfing Bar in Sideways Markets	*125*
The Engulfing Pattern with Supply and Demand Zones	*130*
Money Management Trading Rules	*133*
The Inside Bar Candlestick Pattern	**137**
The Psychology Behind the Inside Bar Pattern Formation	*140*
How to Trade Inside Bars with Support and Resistance	*143*
Tips on Trading the Inside Bar Price Action Setup	*146*
Trading the False Breakout of The Inside Bar Pattern	*148*
Inside bar false breakouts trading examples	*151*
Trading Inside Bar False Breakout with Fibonacci Retracements	*154*
Trades Examples	*158*
Money Management Strategies	*162*
Conclusion	**167**

THE CANDLESTICK TRADING BIBLE

Introduction

The Candlestick trading bible is one of the most powerful trading systems in history. It was invented by Homma Munehisa.The father of candlestick chart patterns.

This trader is considered to be the most successful trader in history, he was known as the God of markets in his days, his discovery made him more than $10 billion in today's dollar.

I have spent 10 years compiling, testing, organizing, and consistently updating this method to create my own new version, which is considered to be the easiest and most profitable trading system.

The Candlestick trading bible is the trading method that is going to finally take your trading to where it should be, consistent, profitable, easy and requiring very little time and effort.

This trading system is based on Japanese candlestick patterns in combination with technical analysis.

All what you have to do is to spend as much time as you can to master the method that i'am going to share with you and use it to trade any financial market.

Learning Japanese candlestick is like learning a new language. Imagine you got a book which is written in a foreign language, you look at the pages but you get nothing from what is written.

The same thing when it comes to financial markets. If you don't know how to read Japanese candlesticks, you will never be able to trade the market.

Japanese candlesticks are the language of financial markets, if you get the skill of reading charts, you will understand what the market is telling you, and you will be able to make the right decision in the right time.

THE CANDLESTICK TRADING BIBLE

The easy to follow strategies detailed in this work will provide you with profit making techniques that can be quickly learned.

More importantly, learning the principals of market psychology underlying the candlestick methodology will change your overall trading psych forever.

The Candlestick trading bible has already proven itself. Fortunes have been made using the Japanese candlestick strategies.

I congratulate you on taking the first step in your trading education, you are on the right path to become a better trader.

However, this is actually just the beginning of your trading career, after finishing this eBook, the real work begins.

Don't read this eBook very fast, this is not a novel, you should take your time to understand all the concepts i discussed, take your notes, and go back from time to time to review the strategies i shared with you.

Remember, this is an educational work that will teach you professional methods on how to make money trading financial markets.

If you got the skills that i shared with you here, you will change completely your life and the life of people around you.

THE CANDLESTICK TRADING BIBLE

Overview

The eBook is divided into the following sections:

1-Candlesticks Anatomy

Just as humans, candlesticks have different body sizes, and when it comes to trading, it's important to check out the bodies of candlesticks and understand the psychology behind it. that's what you will learn in this section.

2-Candlestick patterns

Candlestick patterns are an integral part of technical analysis, candlestick patterns emerge because human actions and reactions are patterned and constantly repeated.

In this section you will learn how to recognize the most important candlestick patterns, the psychology behind it's formation, and what do they indicate when they form in the market.

3-The Market structure

In this section, you will learn how to identify trending markets, ranging markets, and choppy markets. You will learn how these markets move and how to trade them professionally.

You will also learn how to draw support and resistance, and trendlines.

4-Time frames and top down analysis

Multiple time frame analysis is very important for you as a price action trader, in this section you will learn how to analyze the market using the top down analysis approach.

5-Trading strategies and tactics

In this section you will learn how trade the market using four price action trading strategies:

-The pin bar strategy

-The engulfing bar strategy

-The inside bar strategy

-The inside bar false breakout strategy

-Trades examples

I highly recommend you to master the previous sections before jumping to this section, because if you don't master the basics, you will not be able to use these strategies as effective as it would be.

In this section you will learn how to identify high probability setups in the market, and how to use these candlestick patterns in trending markets and ranging markets to maximize your profits.

6-Money management

In this section, you will learn how to create a money management and risk control plan that will allow you to protect your trading capital and become consistently profitable.

THE CANDLESTICK TRADING BIBLE

History of candlesticks

Candlesticks have been around a lot longer than anything similar in the Western world.

The Japanese were looking at charts as far back as the 17th century, whereas the earliest known charts in the US appeared in the late 19th century.

Rice trading had been established in Japan in 1654, with gold, silver and rape seed oil following soon after.

Rice markets dominated Japan at this time and the commodity became, it seems, more important than hard currency.

Munehisa Homma (aka Sokyu Honma), a Japanese rice trader born in the early 1700s, is widely credited as being one of the early exponents of tracking price action.

He understood basic supply and demand dynamics, but also identified the fact that emotion played a part in the setting of price.

He wanted to track the emotion of the market players, and this work became the basis of candlestick analysis.

He was extremely well respected, to the point of being promoted to Samurai status.

The Japanese did an extremely good job of keeping candlesticks quiet from the Western world, right up until the 1980s, when suddenly there was a large cross-pollination of banks and financial institutions around the world.

This is when Westerners suddenly got wind of these mystical charts. Obviously, this was also about the time that charting in general suddenly became a lot easier, due to the widespread use of the PC.

In the late 1980s several Western analysts became interested in candlesticks. In the UK Michael Feeny, who was then head of TA in

London for Sumitomo, began using candlesticks in his daily work, and started introducing the ideas to London professionals.

In the December 1989 edition of Futures magazine Steve Nison, who was a technical analyst at Merrill Lynch in New York, produced a paper that showed a series of candlestick reversal patterns and explained their predictive powers.

He went on to write a book on the subject, and a fine book it is too. Thank you Messrs Feeny and Nison.

Since then candlesticks have gained in popularity by the year, and these days they seem to be the standard template that most analysts work from.

Why candlesticks are important to your trading analysis?

-Candlesticks are important to you trading analysis because, it is considered as a visual representation of what is going on in the market.

By looking at a candlestick, we can get valuable information about the open, high, low and the close of price, which will give us an idea about the price movement.

-Candlesticks are flexible, they can be used alone or in combination with technical analysis tools such as the moving averages, and momentum oscillators, they can be used also with methods such the Dow Theory or the Eliot wave theory.

I personally use candlesticks with support and resistance, trend lines, and other technical tools that you will discover in the next chapters.

-The human behavior in relation to money is always dominated by fear; greed, and hope, candlestick analysis will help us understand these changing psychological factors by showing us how buyers and sellers interact with each other's.

-Candlesticks provide more valuable information than bar charts, using them is a win-win situation, because you can get all the trading signals that bar chart generate with the added clarity and additional signals generated by candlesticks.

-Candlesticks are used by most professional traders, banks, and hedge funds, these guys trade millions of dollars every day, they can move the market whenever they want.

They can take your money easily if you don't understand the game.

Even if you can trade one hundred thousand dollars trading account, you can't move the market; you can't control what is going in the market.

Using candlestick patterns will help you understand what the big boys are doing, and will show you when to enter, when to exit, and when to stay away from the market.

What is a candlestick?

Japanese candlesticks are formed using the open, high, low and close of the chosen time frame.

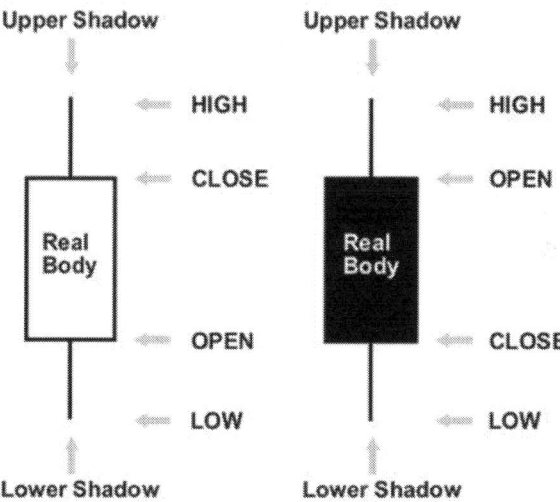

-If the close is above the open, we can say that the candlestick is bullish which means that the market is rising in this period of time. Bullish candlesticks are always displayed as white candlestick.

The most trading platform use white color to refer to bullish candlesticks. But the color doesn't matter, you can use whatever color you want.

The most important is the open price and the close price.

-If the close is below the open, we can say that the candlestick is bearish which indicates that the market is falling in this session. Bearish candles are always displayed as black candlesticks. But this is not a rule.

You can find different colors used to differentiate between bullish and bearish candlesticks.

-The filled part of the candlestick is called the real body.

-The thin lines poking above and below the body are called shadows.

-The top of the upper shadow is the high

-The bottom of the lower shadow is the low.

Candlestick body sizes:

Candlesticks have different body sizes:

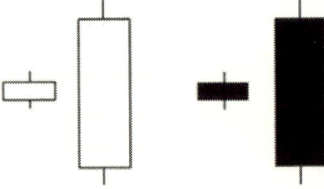

Long bodies refer to strong buying or selling pressure, if there is a candlestick in which the close is above the open with a long body, this indicates that buyers are stronger and they are taking control of the market during this period of time.

Conversely, if there is a bearish candlestick in which the open is above the close with a long body, this means that the selling pressure controls the market during this chosen time frame.

-Short and small bodies indicate a little buying or selling activity.

Candlestick shadows (tails)

The upper and lower shadows give us important information about the trading session.

-Upper shadows signify the session high

-Lower shadows signify the session low

Candlesticks with long shadows show that trading action occurred well past the open and close.

Long Shadows

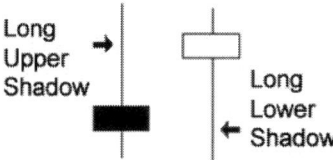

Japanese candlesticks with short shadows indicate that most of the trading action was confined near the open and close.

-If a candlestick has a longer upper shadow, and short lower shadow, this means that buyers flexed their muscles and bid price higher.

But for one reason or another, sellers came in and drove price back down to end the session back near its open price.

-If a Japanese candlestick has a long lower shadow and short upper shadow, this means that sellers flashed their washboard abs and forced price lower. But for one reason or another buyer came in and drove prices back up to end the session back near its' open price.

Candlestick patterns

Candlestick patterns are one of the most powerful trading concepts, they are simple, easy to identify, and very profitable setups, a research has confirmed that candlestick patterns have a high predictive value and can produce positive results.

I personally trade candlestick pattern for more than 20 years; i can't really switch to another method, because i tried thousands of strategies and trading methods with no results.

I'm not going to introduce you to a holy grail, this trading system works, but be prepared to lose some trades, losing is a part of this game, if you are looking for a 100% wining system, i highly recommend you to stop trading and go look for another business.

Candlestick patterns are the language of the market, imagine you are living in a foreign country, and you don't speak the language.

How could you live if you can't even say a word? It's tough right???The same thing when it comes to trading.

If you know how to read candlestick patterns the right way, you will be able to understand what these patterns tell you about the market dynamics and the trader's behavior.

This skill will help you better enter and exit the market in the right time.

In other words, this will help you act differently in the market and make money following the smart guy's footprints.

The candlestick patterns that i'm going to show you here are the most important patterns that you will find in the market, in this chapter, i'm not going to show you how to trade them, because this will be explained in details in the next chapters.

What i want you to do is to focus on the anatomy of the pattern and the psychology behind its formation, because this will help you get the skill of identifying easily any pattern you find in the market and understand what it tells you to do next.

If you can get this skill, you will be ready to understand and master the trading strategies and tactics that i'm going to teach you in the next chapters.

The engulfing bar candlestick pattern

The Engulfing bar as it states in its title is formed when it fully engulfs the previous candle. The engulfing bar can engulf more than one previous candle, but to be considered an engulfing bar, at least one candle must be fully consumed.

The bearish engulfing is one of the most important candlestick patterns.

This candlestick pattern consists of two bodies:

The first body is smaller than the second one, in other words, the second body engulfs the previous one. See the illustration below:

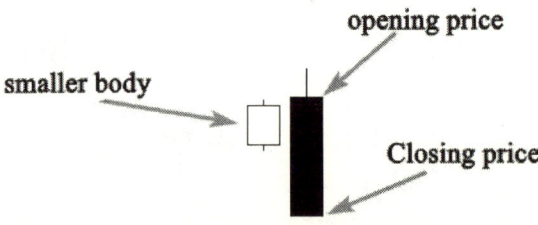

This is how a bearish engulfing bar pattern looks like on your charts, this candlestick pattern gives us valuable information about bulls and bears in the market.

In case of a bearish engulfing bar, this pattern tells us that sellers are in control of the market.

When this pattern occurs at the end of an uptrend, this indicates that buyers are engulfed by sellers which signals a trend reversal.

See the example below:

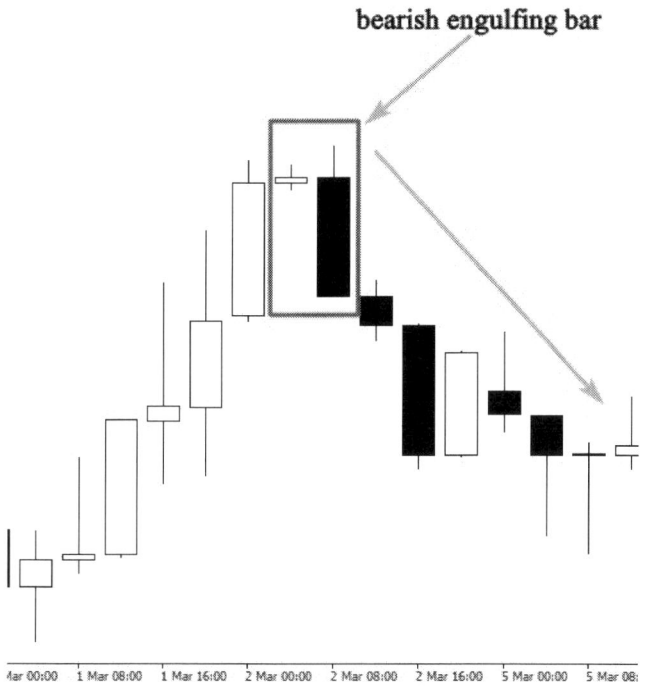

As you can see when this price action pattern occurs in an uptrend, we can anticipate a trend reversal because buyers are not still in control of the market, and sellers are trying to push the market to go down.

You can't trade any bearish candlestick pattern you find on your chart; you will need other technical tools to confirm your entries.

We will talk about this in details in the next chapters. Right now, i just want you to open your charts and try to identify all bearish candlestick patterns that you find.

The bullish engulfing bar pattern

The bullish engulfing bar consists of two candlesticks, the first one is the small body, and the second is the engulfing candle,

see the illustration:

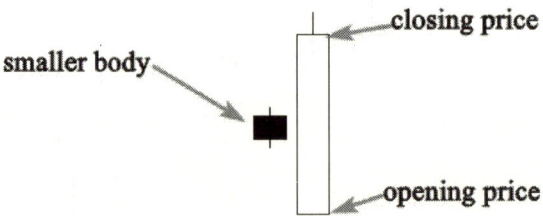

The bullish engulfing bar pattern tells us that the market is no longer under control of sellers, and buyers will take control of the market.

When a bullish engulfing candle forms in the context of an uptrend, it indicates a continuation signal.

When a bullish engulfing candle forms at the end of a downtrend, the reversal is much more powerful as it represents a capitulation bottom. See the example below:

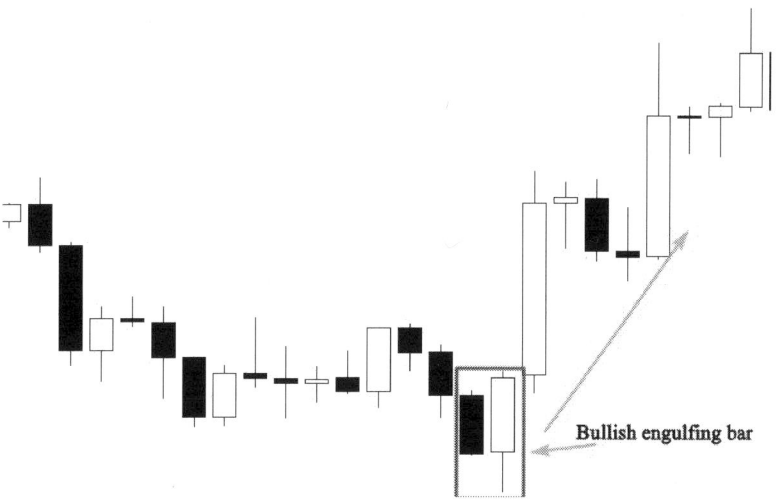

Bullish engulfing bar

The example above shows us clearly how the market changes direction after the formation of a bullish engulfing bar pattern.

The smaller body that represents the selling power was covered by the second body that represents the buying power.

The color of the bodies is not important. What's important is that the smaller one is totally engulfed by the second candlestick.

Don't try to trade the market using this price action setup alone, because you will need other factors of confluence to decide whether the pattern is worth trading or not, i will talk about this in the next chapters.

What i want you to do now is to get the skill of identifying bearish and bullish engulfing bar on your charts. This is the most important step for the moment.

The Doji Candlestick pattern

Doji is one of the most important Japanese candlestick patterns, when this candlestick forms, it tells us that the market opens and closes at the same price which means that there is equality and indecision between buyers and sellers, there is no one in control of the market. See the example below:

Doji Candlestick

Highest price

closing price *opening price*

lowest price

As you can see the opening price is the same as the closing price, this signal means that the market didn't decide which direction will take. When this pattern occurs in an uptrend or a downtrend, it indicates that the market is likely to reverse.

See another example below to learn more:

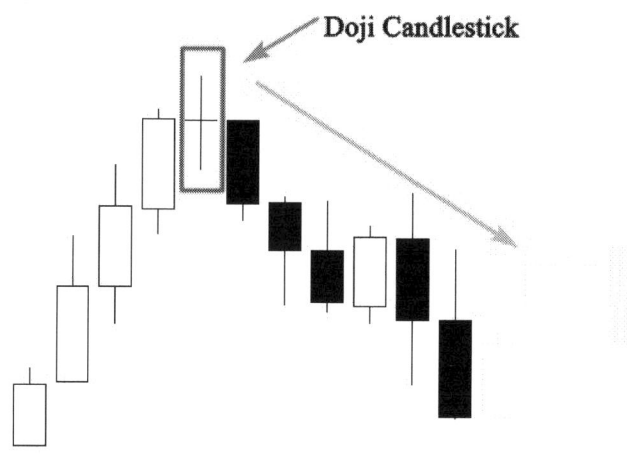

The chart above shows how the market changed direction after the formation of the Doji candlestick.

The market was trending up, that means that buyers were in control of the market.

The formation of the Doji candlestick indicates that buyers are unable to keep price higher, and sellers push prices back to the opening price.

This is a clear indication that a trend reversal is likely to happen.

Remember always that a Doji indicates equality and indecision in the market, you will often find it during periods of resting after big moves higher or lower.

When it is found at the bottom or at the top of a trend, it is considered as a sign that a prior trend is losing its strengths.

So if you are already riding that trend it's time to take profits, it can also be used as an entry signal if it is combined with other technical analysis

The Dragonfly Doji pattern

The Dragonfly Doji is a bullish candlestick pattern which is formed when the open high and close are the same or about the same price.

What characterizes the dragonfly Doji is the long lower tail that shows the resistance of buyers and their attempt to push the market up.

See the example below:

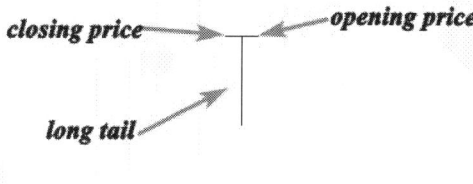

The illustration above shows us a prefect dragonfly Doji. The long lower tail suggests that the forces of supply and demand are nearing a balance and that the direction of the trend may be nearing a major turning point.

See the example below that indicates a bullish reversal signal created by a dragonfly Doji.

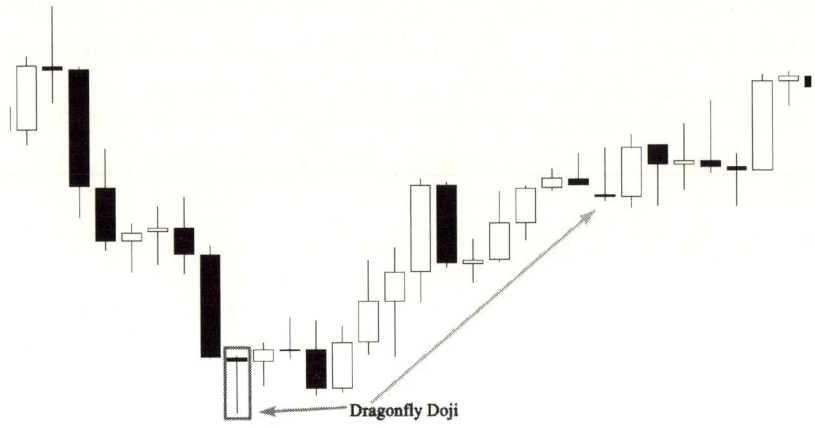

In the chart above, the market was testing the previous support level that caused a strong rejection from this area.

The formation of the dragonfly Doji with the long lower tail shows us that there is a high buying pressure in the area.

If you can identify this candlestick pattern on your chart, it will help you visually see when support and demand are located.

When it occurs in a downtrend, it is interpreted as a bullish reversal signal.

But as i always say, you can't trade candlestick pattern alone, you will need other indicators and tools to determine high probability dragonfly Doji signals in the market.

The Gravestone Doji

The Gravestone Doji is the bearish version of the dragonfly Doji, it is formed when the open and close are the same or about the same price.

What differentiates the Gravestone Doji from the dragonfly Doji is the long upper tail.

The formation of the long upper tail is an indication that the market is testing a powerful supply or resistance area.

See the example below:

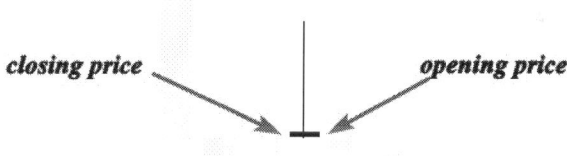

The image above illustrates a perfect gravestone Doji. This pattern indicates that while buyers were able to push prices well above the open.

Later in the day sellers overwhelmed the market pushing the price back down.

This is interpreted as a sign that bulls are losing their momentum and the market is ready for a reversal.

See another illustration below:

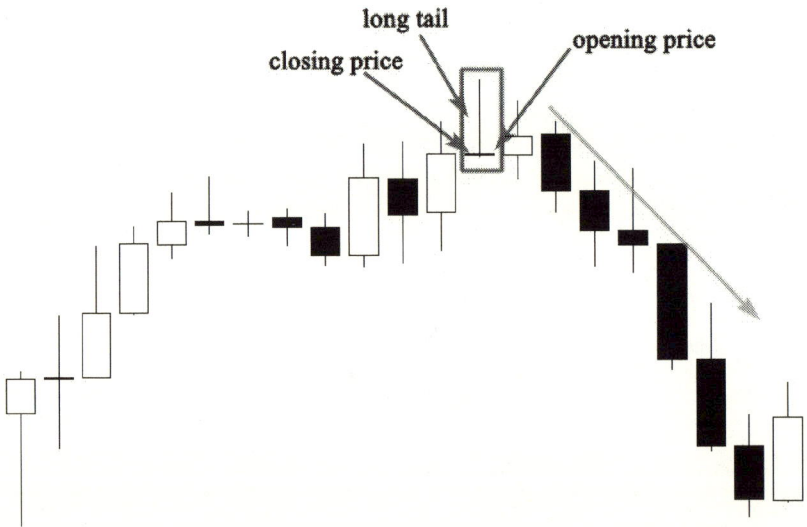

The chart above shows a gravestone Doji at the top of an uptrend, after a period of strong bullish activity.

The formation of this candlestick pattern indicates that buyers are no longer in control of the market. For this pattern to be reliable, it must occur near a resistance level.

As a trader, you will need additional information about the placement and context of the gravestone Doji to interpret the signal effectively. This is what i will teach you in the next chapters.

The morning star

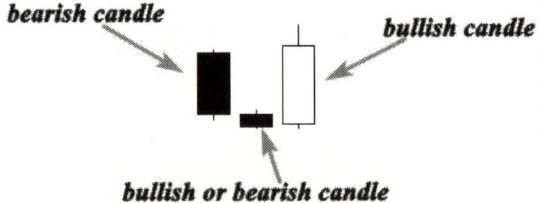

The morning star pattern is considered as a bullish reversal pattern, it often occurs at the bottom of a downtrend and it consists of three candlesticks:

-The first candlestick is bearish which indicates that sellers are still in charge of the market.

-The second candle is a small one which represents that sellers are in control, but they don't push the market much lower and this candle can be bullish or bearish.

-The third candle is a bullish candlestick that gapped up on the open and closed above the midpoint of the body of the first day, this candlestick holds a significant trend reversal signal.

The morning star pattern shows us how buyers took control of the market from sellers, when this pattern occurs at the bottom of downtrend near a support level, it is interpreted as a powerful trend reversal signal.

See the illustration below:

The chart above helps us identify the morning star pattern and how it is significant when it is formed at the bottom of a downtrend.

As you can see the pattern occurred at an obvious bearish trend.

The first candle confirmed the seller's domination, and the second one produces indecision in the market, the second candle could be a Doji, or any other candle.

But here, the Doji candle indicated that sellers are struggling to push the market lower. The third bullish candle indicates that buyers took control from sellers, and the market is likely to reverse.

This is how professional traders analyze the market based on candlestick patterns, and this is how you will analyze financial markets if you can master the anatomy of candlestick patterns and the psychology behind their formations.

The evening star pattern

The evening star pattern is considered as a bearish reversal pattern that usually occurs at the top of an uptrend.

The pattern consists of three candlesticks:

-The first candle is a bullish candle

-The second candle is a small candlestick, it can be bullish or bearish or it can be a Doji or any other candlestick.

-The third candle is a large bearish candle. In general, the evening star pattern is the bearish version of the morning star pattern. See the example below:

The evening star candlestick pattern

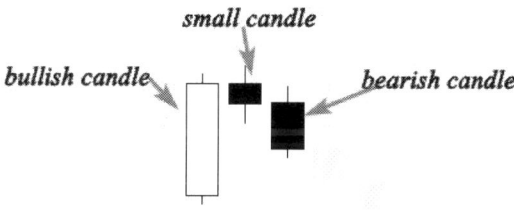

The first part of an evening star is a bullish candle; this means that bulls are still pushing the market higher.

Right now, everything is going all right. The formation of the smaller body shows that buyers are still in control but they are not as powerful as they were.

The third bearish candle indicates that the buyer's domination is over, and a possible bearish trend reversal is likely to happen.

See another chart that illustrates how the evening star could represent a significant trend reversal signal.

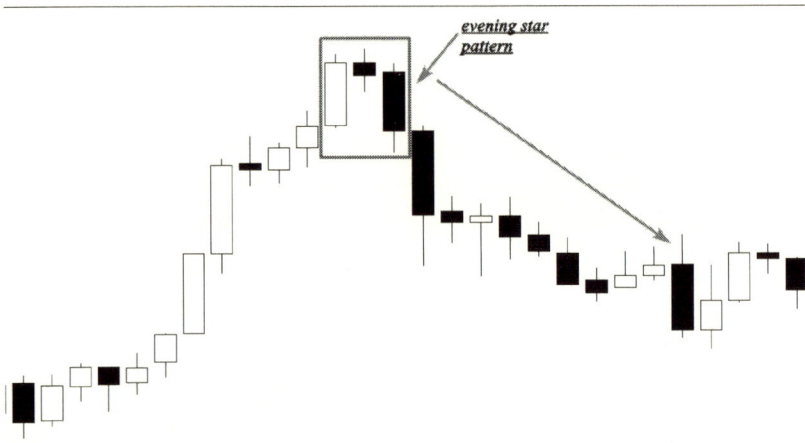

As you can see the market was trending up, the first candle in the pattern indicates a long move up.

The second one is a short candle indicating price consolidation and indecision.

In other words, the trend that created the first long bullish candlestick is losing momentum. The final candlestick gaping lower than the previous candlestick indicating a confirmation of the reversal and the beginning of a new trend down.

THE CANDLESTICK TRADING BIBLE

The Hammer (pin bar)

The Hammer candlestick is created when the open high and close are roughly the same price; it is also characterized by a long lower shadow that indicates a bullish rejection from buyers and their intention to push the market higher.

See the illustration below to see how it looks like:

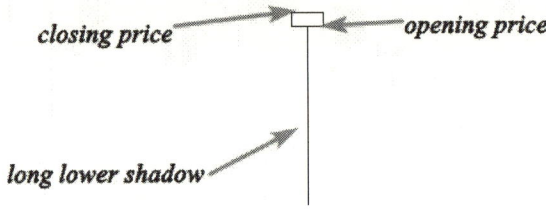

The hammer is a reversal candlestick pattern when it occurs at the bottom of a downtrend.

This candle forms when sellers push the market lower after the open, but they get rejected by buyers so the market closes higher than the lowest price.

See another example below:

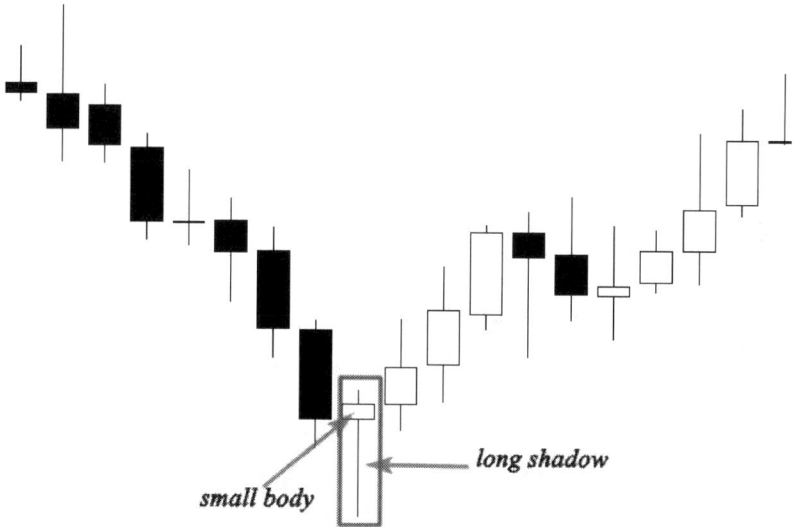

As you can see the market was trending down, the formation of the hammer (pin bar) was a significant reversal pattern.

The long shadow represents the high buying pressure from this point.

Sellers was trying to push the market lower, but in that level the buying power was more powerful than the selling pressure which results in a trend reversal.

The most important to understand is the psychology behind the formation of this pattern, if you can understand how and why it was created, you will be able to predict the market direction with high accuracy.

We will talk about how to trade this pattern and how to filter this signal in the next chapters.

The shooting star (bearish pin bar)

The shooting formation is formed when the open low, and close are roughly the same price, this candle is characterized by a small body

and a long upper shadow. It is the bearish version of the hammer. Professional technicians say that the shadow should be twice the length of the real body.

See the example below:

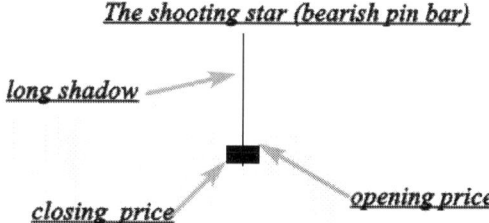

The illustration above shows us a perfect shooting star with a real small body and an upper long shadow, when this pattern occurs in an uptrend; it indicates a bearish reversal signal.

The psychology behind the formation of this pattern is that buyers try to push the market higher, but they got rejected by a selling pressure.

When this candlestick forms near a resistance level. It should be taken as a high probability setup.

See another example below:

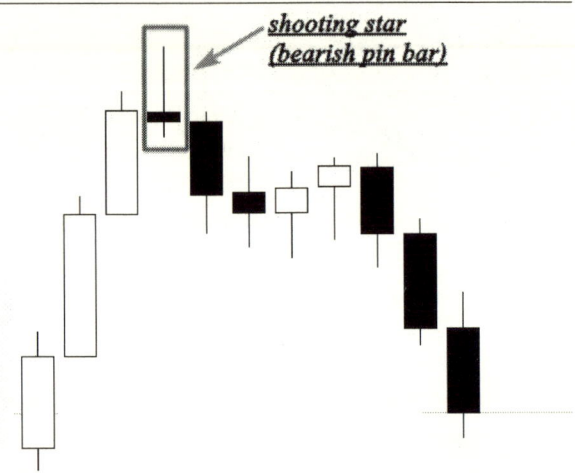

The chart above shows a nice shooting star at the end of an uptrend.

The formation of this pattern indicates the end of the uptrend move, and the beginning of a new downtrend.

This candlestick pattern can be used with support and resistance, supply and demand areas, and with technical indicators.

The shooting star is very easy to identify, and it is very profitable, it is one of the most powerful signals that i use to enter the market.

In the next chapters, i will talk about it in details, and i will show you step by step how to make money trading this price action pattern.

The Harami Pattern (the inside bar)

The Harami pattern (pregnant in Japanese) is considered as a reversal and continuation pattern, and it consists of two candlesticks:

The first candle is the large candle, it is called the mother candle, followed by a smaller candle which is called the baby.

For the Harami pattern to be valid, the second candle should close outside the previous one.

This candlestick is considered as a bearish reversal signal when it occurs at the top of an uptrend, and it is a bullish signal when it occurs at the bottom of a downtrend.

See an example below:

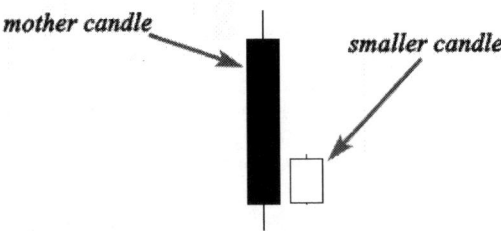

Harami pattern bullish inside bar

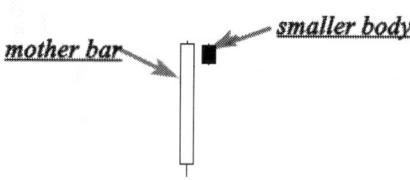

As you see the smaller body is totally covered by the previous mother candle, don't bother yourself with the colors, the most important is that the smaller body closes inside of the first bigger candle.

The Harami candle tells us that the market is in an indecision period. In other words, the market is consolidating.

So, buyers and sellers don't know what to do, and there is no one in control of the market.

When this candlestick pattern happens during an uptrend or a downtrend, it is interpreted as a continuation pattern which gives a good opportunity to join the trend.

And if it is occurred at the top of an uptrend or at the bottom of a downtrend, it is considered as a trend reversal signal.

Look at another example below:

THE CANDLESTICK TRADING BIBLE

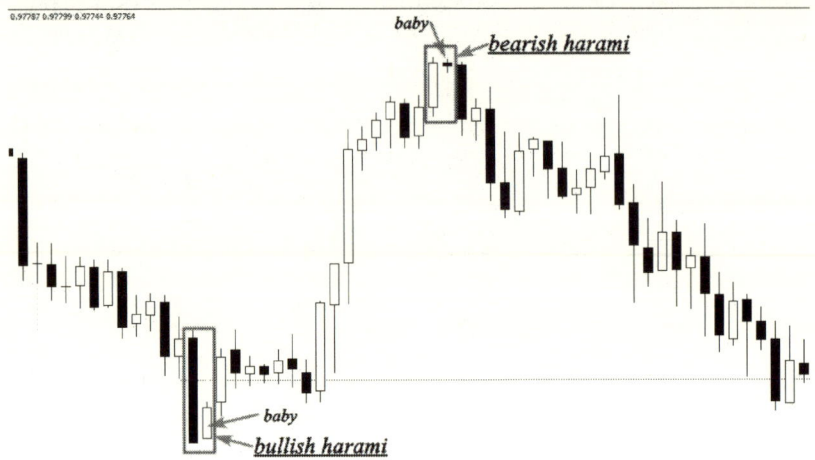

In the chart above, you can see how the trend direction changes after the Harami pattern formation, the first bullish harami pattern occurred at the bottom of a downtrend, sellers were pushing the market lower, suddenly price starts consolidating, and this indicates that the selling power is no longer in control of the market.

The bearish Harami is the opposite of the bullish, this one occurred at the top of an uptrend indicating that buyer's domination is over and the beginning of a downtrend is possible.

When this pattern is created during an uptrend or a downtrend, it indicates a continuation signal with the direction of the market.

We will study in details how to trade this pattern either as a reversal pattern or as a continuation pattern in the next chapters.

The Tweezers tops and bottoms

The tweezers top formation is considered as a bearish reversal pattern seen at the top of an uptrend, and the tweezers bottom formation is interpreted as a bullish reversal pattern seen at the bottom of a downtrend.

See the example below:

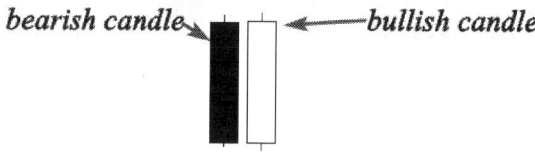

Twezzer Top

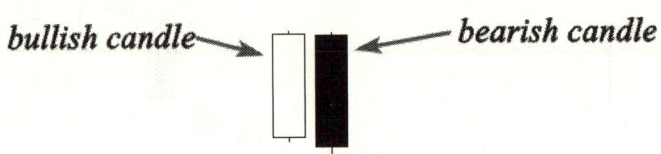

The tweezers top formation consists of two candlesticks:

The first one is a bullish candlestick followed by a bearish candlestick. And the tweezers bottom formation consists of two candlesticks as well.

The first candle is bearish followed by a bullish candlestick.

So we can say that the tweezers bottom is the bullish version of the tweezers top.

The tweezers top occurs during an uptrend when buyers push the price higher, this gave us the impression that the market is still going up, but sellers surprised buyers by pushing the market lower and close down the open of the bullish candle.

This price action pattern indicates a bullish trend reversal and we can trade it if we can combine this signal with other technical tools.

The tweezers bottom happens during a downtrend, when sellers push the market lower, we feel that everything is going all right, but the next session price closes above or roughly at the same price of the first bearish candle which indicates that buyers are coming to reverse the market direction.

If this price action happens near a support level, it indicates that a bearish reversal is likely to happen.

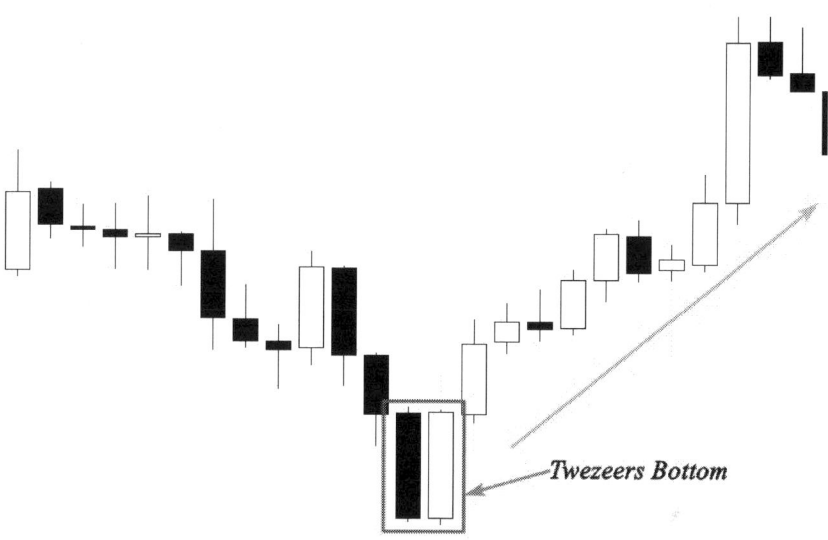

The chart above shows us a tweezers bottom that occurs in a downtrend, the bears pushed the market downward on the first session; however, the second session opened where prices closed on the first session and went straight up indicating a reversal buy signal that you can trade if you have other elements that confirm your buying decision.

Don't focus on the name of a candlestick, try to understand the psychology behind its formation, this is the most important.

Because if you can understand why it was formed, you will understand what happened in the market, and you can easily predict the future movement of price.

THE CANDLESTICK TRADING BIBLE

Candlestick patterns exercise

Now i think that you get some information about Japanese candlesticks, you know the anatomy of each candlestick and the psychology behind its formation, let' take this exercise to test your knowledge and see if you still remember all of the candlesticks we talked about.

Look at the chart below and try to find the name of each candlestick number, and the psychology behind its formation.

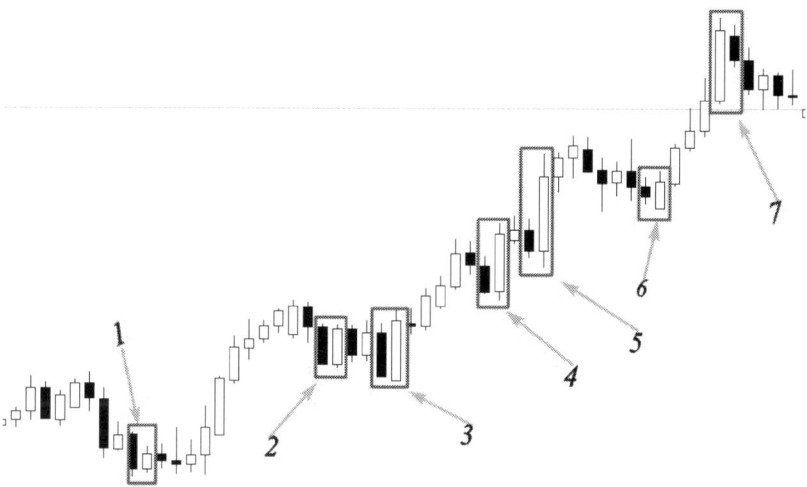

If you can easily identify these candlestick patterns, and you understand why they are formed. You are on the right path.

But if you still struggle to identify these patterns, you will have to start learning about them again till you feel like you master them.

Let's try to answer the questions concerning the candlestick patterns on the charts above:

1: Bullish Harami pattern (inside bar)

-The formation of this candlestick patterns indicates indecision in the market, in other words, the market was consolidating during this session.

2: Bullish Tweezers

The market was trading up, sellers tried to push the market lower, but the reaction of buyers was more powerful.

This pattern represents the battle between sellers and buyers to take control of the market.

3: Engulfing bar

-Sellers were engulfed by buyers, this indicates that buyers are still willing to push the market higher.

4: Engulfing bar

5: Engulfing bar

6: Engulfing bar

7: Harami pattern

This pattern shows us that the market enters in a consolidation phase during this session.so buyers and sellers are in an indecision period. And no one knows who is going to be in control of the market.

THE CANDLESTICK TRADING BIBLE

Let's take another exercise, look at the chart below and try to figure out these candlestick patterns:

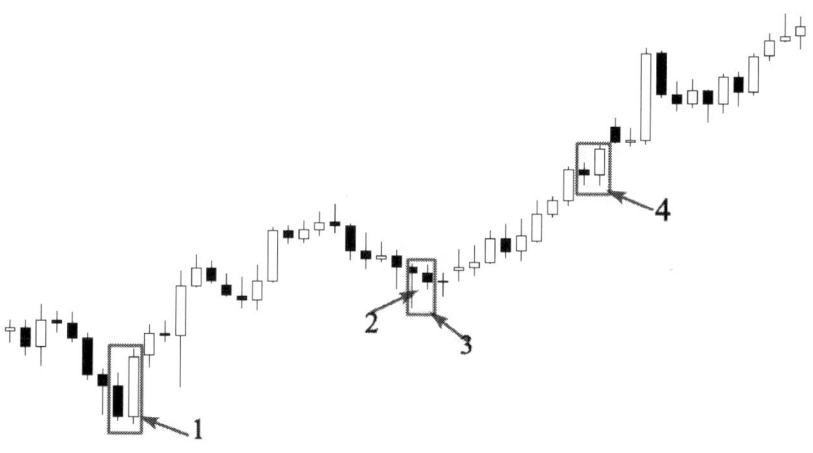

Answers:

1: Bullish engulfing bar

2: Hammer

3:(Hammer which is the large body +the smaller body (baby) =Harami pattern

4: Bullish engulfing bar

Please, i want you to open your charts, and do this homework over and over again. You will see that with screen time and practice, you will be able to look at your charts, and understand what the candlesticks tell you about the market.

Don't worry about how to enter and exit the market for the moment, take your time and try to master the candlestick patterns discussed in the previous chapters.

In the next chapters, i will arm you with techniques that will help you identify the best entry and exit points based on candlestick patterns in combination with technical analysis.

Trust me, these price action strategies will turn you from a beginner trader who struggles to make money in the market into a profitable price action trader.

The market structure

One of the most important skill that you need as a trader is the ability to read the market structure, it is a critical skill that will allow you to use the right price action strategies in the right market condition.

You are not going to trade all the markets the same way; you need to study how the markets move, and how traders behave in the market. The market structure is the study of the market behavior.

And if you can master this skill, when you open your chart, you will be able to answer these important questions:

What the crowds are doing? Who is in control of the market buyers or sellers? What is the right time and place to enter or to exit the market and when you need to stay away?

Through your price action analysis, you will experience three types of markets, trending markets, ranging markets, and choppy markets.

In this chapter, you will learn how to identify every market, and how to trade it.

1-Trending markets

Trending markets are simply characterized by a repeating pattern of higher highs and higher low in an up-trending market, and lower high and lower low in a down trending market.

See the example below:

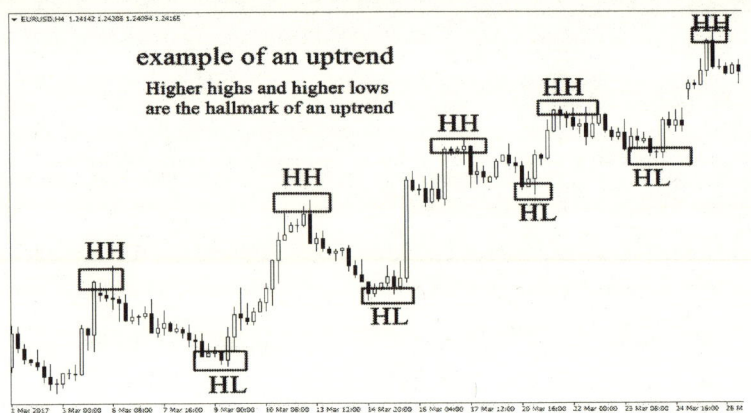

As you can see in the example above, the market is making series of higher highs and higher lows which indicates that the market is up trending.

You don't need indicators to decide if it is bullish or bearish just a visual observation of price action is quite enough to get an idea about the market trend.

Look another example of a downtrend market.

The example above shows a bearish market, as you can see there are series of higher lows and lower low which indicate an obvious downtrend.

Trending markets are easy to identify, don't try to complicate your analysis, use your brain and see what the market is doing.

If it is doing series of higher highs and higher low, it is simply an uptrend market; conversely, if it is making series of lower highs and lower low, it is obviously a downtrend market.

-According to statistics, trends are estimated to occur 30% of the time, so while they are in motion, you've got to know how to take advantage of them.

-To determine whether a market is trending or not, you have to use bigger time frames such the 4H, the daily or the weekly time frame. Never try to use smaller time frames to determine the market structure.

How to trade trending markets:

If you can identify a trending market, it will be easy for you to trade it, if it is a bullish market, you will look for a buying opportunity, because you have to trade with the trend, and if the market is bearish, you have to look for a selling opportunity.

But the question is what is the right time to enter a trending market?

Trending markets are characterized by two important moves, the first move is called, the impulsive move, and the second one is called the retracement move.

See the example below to understand what i'm talking about.

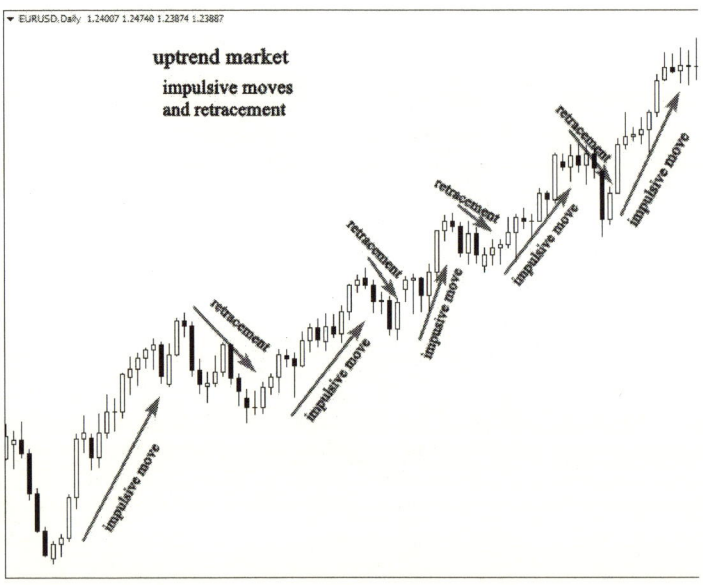

As you can see, the market is making higher highs and higher lows which indicates a bullish market, if you see this market you will think of buying. But as you can see the market is making two different moves, the first move is an impulsive move, and the second one is a pullback or a retracement move. (corrective move)

Professional traders understand how trending markets move; they always buy at the beginning of an impulsive move and take profits at the end of it.

This is the reason why the market makes an impulsive move in the direction of the trend and retraces before it makes another impulsive move.

If you are aware of how trending markets move, you will know that the best place to buy is at the beginning of an impulsive move, traders who buy an uptrend market at the beginning of a retracement move, they got caught by professional traders, and they don't understand why the market hint their stop loss before moving in the predicted direction. See another example of a bearish trend.

THE CANDLESTICK TRADING BIBLE

The illustration above shows a downtrend market, as you can see the best trading decision is to sell the market at the beginning of an impulsive move.

If you try to sell in the retracement move, you will be trapped by professional traders, and you will lose your trade.

Now we know how to identify downtrends and uptrends, and how to differentiate between an impulsive move, and a retracement move. This is very important for you as a price action trader to know.

BUT the most important question is how to identify the beginning of the impulsive move to enter the market in the right time with professional traders, and avoid being trapped by the retracement move?

To predict the beginning of the impulsive move in a trending market, you have to master drawing support and resistance levels.

So, what are support and resistance levels and how to draw them on our charts? this is what we will see in the next chapter.

Support and Resistance levels

Support and resistance are proven areas where buyers and sellers find some of equilibrium, they are major turning points in the market.

Support and resistance levels are formed when price reverses and change direction, and price will often respect these support and resistance levels, in other words, they tend to contain price movement until of course price breaks through them.

In trending markets, support and resistance are formed from swing points. in an uptrend the previous swing point acts as a support level, and in a downtrend the old swing point acts as a resistance level.

See the example below to learn more

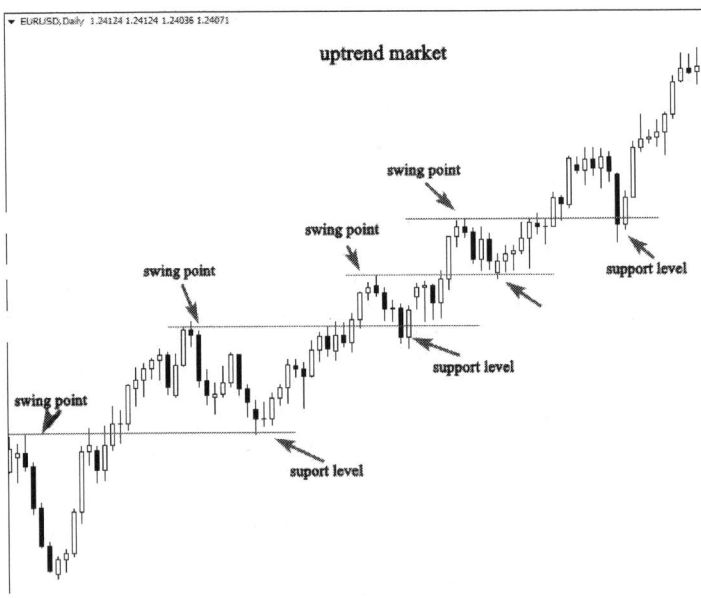

THE CANDLESTICK TRADING BIBLE

The illustration above shows how the previous swing point acts as a support level after the breakout.

When the market makes the retracement move it respects the previous swing point (support level) which will represent the beginning of another impulsive move.

As you can see, when the market tests the previous swing point (support level) it goes up again.

By drawing a support level in an uptrend market, we can predict when the next impulsive move will take place.

Let's see another example of a downtrend market.

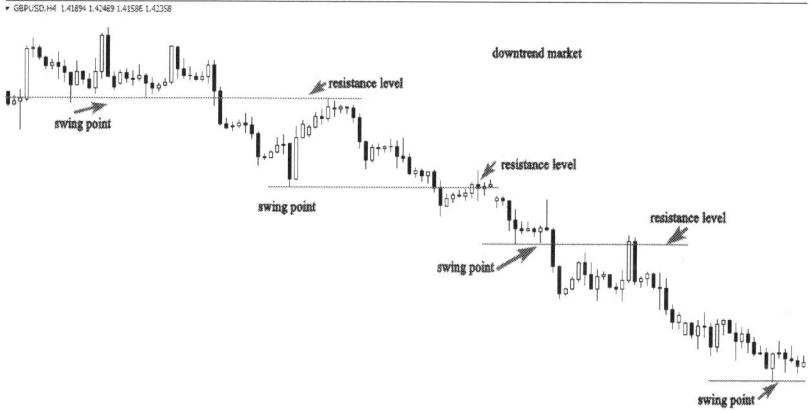

The illustration above shows us how the market respects resistance levels, when price approach the previous swing point, (resistance level).

The market makes an impulsive move. If you understand how price action act in a trending market, you will predict with high accuracy when the next impulsive move will begin.

Another way to catch the beginning of an impulsive move is by drawing trend lines.

This is another technical skill that you have to learn if you want to identify key linear support and resistance level.

Let me explain you first what do trend lines mean?

Quite often when the market is on the move making new swing highs and lows, price will tend to respect a linear level which is identified as a trend line.

Bullish markets will tend to create a linear support level, and bearish markets will form a linear resistance level.

How to draw trend lines?

To draw a quality trend line, you will need to find at least 2 minimum swing points, and simply connect them with each other. The levels must be clear, don't try to force a trend line.

Don't use smaller time frame to draw trend lines, use always the 4H and the daily time frames to find obvious trend lines.

We will try to focus right now on how to draw them in a trending markets, our purpose is to identify the beginning of impulsive moves in a trending market.

In the next chapter, i will explain you in detail how to trade trend lines in combination with our price action trading setups.

See an example of how to draw trend lines in a downtrend market.

As you can see the market respects the trend line, and when price approach it, the market reverse and continue in the same direction.

When the market moves this way, trend lines help us to anticipate the next impulsive move with the direction of the market.

Look at another example of an uptrend market.

As you can see the market respects the trend line, and by drawing it the right way, we can easily predict the next movement upward.

This is all what we can say about trending markets, i think it's clear and simple, now what i want you to do is to open your charts and try to find trending markets.

Find previous swing points (support and resistance).and try to find trend lines as well.

This exercise will help you understand how trending markets move. And how to predict high probability entries in the market.

The Ranging Market

Ranging markets are pretty straight forward, they are often called sideways markets, because their neutral nature makes them appear to drift to the right, horizontally.

When the market makes a series of higher highs and higher lows, we can say that the market is trending up.

But when it stops making these consecutive peaks, we say that the market is ranging.

A ranging market moves in a horizontal form, where buyers and sellers just keep knocking price back and forth between the support and the resistance level.

See the example below:

The chart above shows a ranging market, as you can see, the price is bouncing between horizontal support and resistance level.

The difference between trending markets and ranging markets is that trending markets tend to move by forming a pattern of higher high and higher lows in case of an uptrend, and higher low and lower low in case of a downtrend.

But ranging markets tend to move horizontally between key support and resistance levels.

Your understanding of the difference between the both markets will help you better use the right price action strategies in the right market conditions.

Trading ranging markets is completely different from trading trending markets, because when the market is ranging, it creates equilibrium, buyers are equal to sellers, and there is no one in control.

This will generally continue until the range structures broke out , and a trending condition start to organize.

The best buying and selling opportunities occur at key support and resistance levels.

There are three ways to trade ranging markets, i'm not going to go into details, because what i want you to get here is the skill to look at your charts and decide whether the market is trending or ranging.

In the next chapters i will go into details and i will give the trading tactics and strategies that you will use to trade trending or ranging markets.

If you can't differentiate between ranging markets and trending markets, you will not know how to use these price action strategies.

The first way to trade ranging markets is by waiting for price to approach support or resistance level then you can buy at key support level and sell at key resistance level.

See the example below:

As you can see, the market is moving horizontally, in this case the best buying opportunities occur at the support level.

And the best selling opportunities occur at the resistance level.

The second way of trading ranging markets is by waiting for the breakout from either the support level or the resistance level.

When the market is ranging, no one knows what is going to happen, we don't know who is going to be in control of the market, this is why you have to pay attention to the boundaries, but when one of the players decide to take control of the market, we will see a breakout of the support or the resistance level.

The breakout means that the ranging period is over, and the beginning of a new trend will take place...

See the example below:

THE CANDLESTICK TRADING BIBLE

As you can see the market was trading between support and resistance levels, and suddenly the price broke out of the resistance level, this indicates that the beginning of a trend is likely to happen.

So the best way to enter is after the breakout.

It's important to remember that range boundaries are often overshot, giving the illusion a breakout is occurring, this can be very deceptive, and it does trap a lot of traders who positioned into the breakout.

The third way to trade ranging markets is to wait for a pullback after the breakout of the support or the resistance level.

The pullback is another chance to join the trend for traders who didn't enter in the breakout.

See the example below:

As you can see in the chart above, the market was ranging, price breaks out of the resistance level to indicate the end of the ranging period, and the beginning of a new trend.

After the breakout, the market comes back to retest the resistance level that becomes support before it goes up.

The pullback is your second chance to join the buyers if you miss the breakout.

But Pullbacks don't always occur after every breakout, when it occurs, it represents a great opportunity with a good risk to reward ratio.

What you have to remember is that a ranging market moves horizontally between the support and the resistance level.

These are the key levels that you have to focus on. The breakout of the support or the resistance level indicates that the ranging period is over, so you have to make sure that the breakout is real to join the new trend safely.

If you miss the breakout, wait for the pullback. when it occurs, don't hesitate to enter the market.

When you are trading ranging markets, always make sure that the market is worth trading, if you feel like you can't identify the boundaries (support and resistance). this is a clear indication of a choppy market.

In Forex, choppy markets are those which have no clear directions, when you open your chart, and you find a lot of noise, you can't even decide if the market is ranging, or trending.

You have to know that you are watching a choppy market. This type of markets can make you feel very emotional and doubt your trading strategies as it starts to drop in performance.

The best way to determine if a market is choppy is just by zooming out on the daily chart and taking in the bigger picture.

After some training, screen time and experience, you will easily be able to identify if a market is ranging or it is a choppy market.

Here is a good example of a choppy chart that is not worth trading.

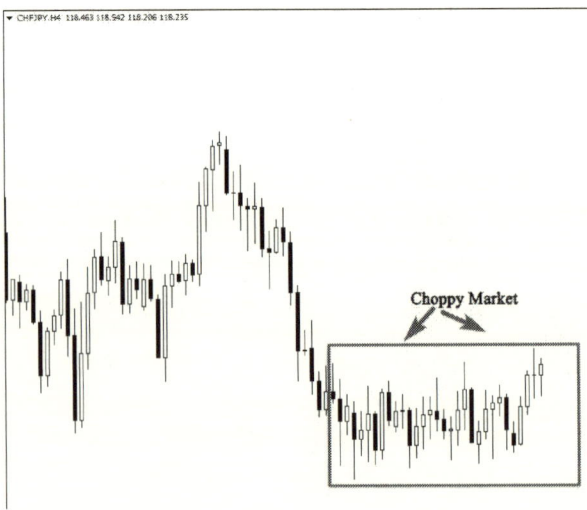

Notice in the chart above, the price action in the highlighted area is very choppy, and it is moving sideways in a very small tight range. This is a sign of a choppy market that you should stay away from.

If a market is choppy, in my opinion, it is not worth trading, if you try to trade it, you will give back your profits shortly after big winners, because markets often consolidate after making big moves.

Time frames and top down analysis

As a price action trader, your primary time frame is the 1H, the 4H and the daily.

Price action works on bigger time frames, if you try to trade pin bars or engulfing bars on the 5-minute time frame, you will lose your money, because there is lot of noise on smaller time frames, and the market will generate lot of false signals because of the hard battle between the bears and bulls.

Besides, there is no successful price action trader who focuses on one-time frame to analyze his charts, maybe you have heard of the term top and down analysis which means to begin with bigger time frames to get the big picture, and then you switch to the smaller one to decide whether to buy or to sell the market.

Let's say you want to trade the 4h chart, you have to look at the weekly chart first, and then the daily chart, if the weekly and the daily charts analysis align with the 4h chart, you can then take your trading decision.

And if you want to trade the 1H chart, you have to look at the daily chart first. This is a critical step to do as a price action trader, because this will help you avoid low probability trading setups, and it will allow you to stay focused on high probability price action signals.

Through our top down analysis, we always start with the bigger time frame, and we look for to gather the following information:

-**The most important support and resistance levels:** these areas represent turning points in the market, if you can identify them on the weekly chart, you will know what is going to happen when the price approaches these levels on the 4h chart.

So you will decide either to buy, to sell or to ignore the signals you get from the market.

-The market structure: the weekly analysis will help you identify if the market is trending up or down, or it is ranging, or choppy market. In general, you will know what the big investors are doing. And you will try to find a way to follow them on the smaller time frames using my price action strategies.

-The previous candle: the last candle on the weekly chart is important, because it tells us what happens during a week, and it provides us with valuable information about the future market move.

When you identify these points using the weekly chart, you can now move to the daily chart or the 4h chart and try to gather information such as:

-The market condition: what the market is doing on the 4h time frame, is it trending up or down, is it ranging, or is it a choppy market.

- what are the most important key levels on the 4h or the daily time frame: this could be support and resistance, supply and demand areas, trend lines….

-price action signal: a candlestick patterns that will provide you with a signal to buy or short the market. This could be a pin bar, an engulfing bar or an inside bar…

Let me give you an example to help you understand why it is important to adopt the top down analysis concept in your trading method and what is going to happen if you don't look at the bigger time frame before switching to your primary chart.

Look at the illustration below:

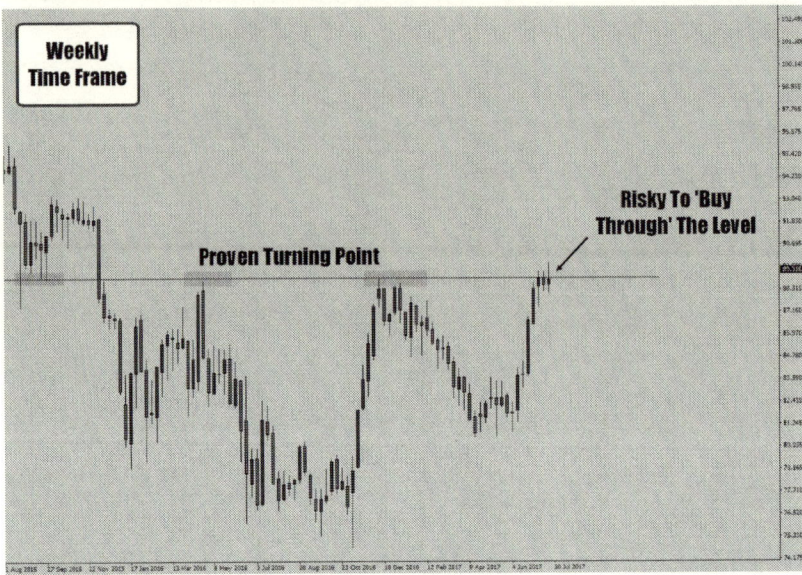

As you can see in this weekly chart above, we have gathered two important points that will help us decide what to do on the daily time frame.

The first point is that the market approaches to an important weekly resistance level that will represent a hot point in the market.

The second information is the rejection from this key resistance level, as you can see the price was rejected immediately when it approaches the level, this indicates that there are sellers there and they are willing to short the market.

What confirms our analysis is the formation of the inside bar false breakout patterns that indicates a reversal.

Now let's switch to the daily time frame to see what is going on in the market:

THE CANDLESTICK TRADING BIBLE

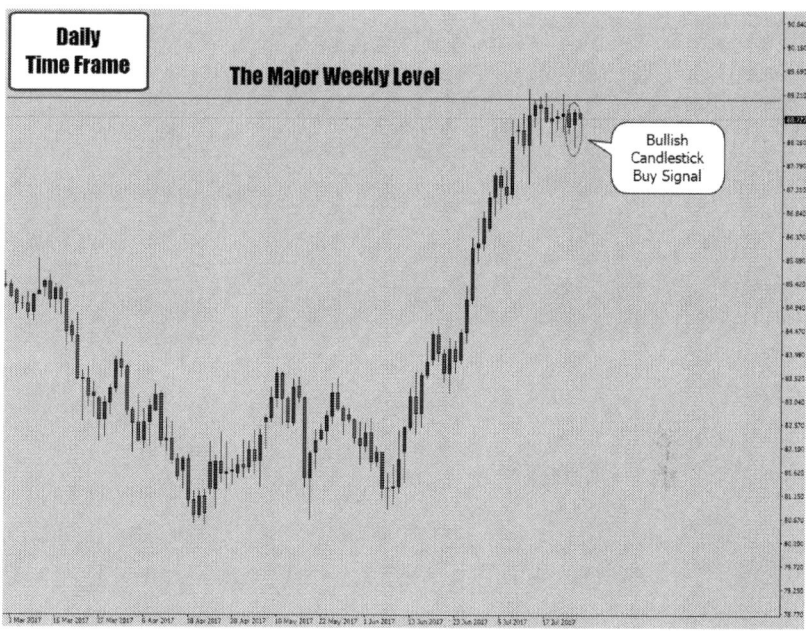

On the daily chart, we have a clear pin bar candlestick pattern that indicates a bullish signal.

if you focus just on one-time frame to make your trading decision,

You will buy the market, because there is a clear pin bar signal.

But if you analyzed the weekly chart, you would know that there is a very powerful key level that will stop the market from going up.

So, it's better to think of selling the market if there is a clear signal rather than to buy it.

Look at what happened next:

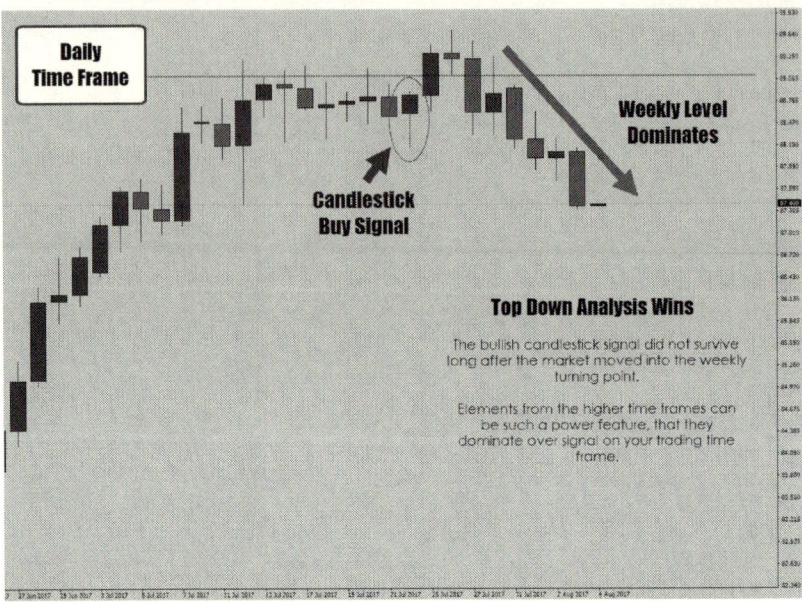

As you can see, the top down analysis works, the pin bar candlestick signal didn't work, because the weekly resistance level was a powerful turning point that reversed the market direction.

If you want to trade price action based on one-time frame, i highly recommend you to stop trading because you will end up losing your entire trading account, and you will never become a successful trader.

Trading counter trends is very profitable as well, but without the top down analysis, you will put yourself in troubles.

Let me give you another example to show how you can trade counter trends using your price action trading setups in combination with the top down analysis concept.

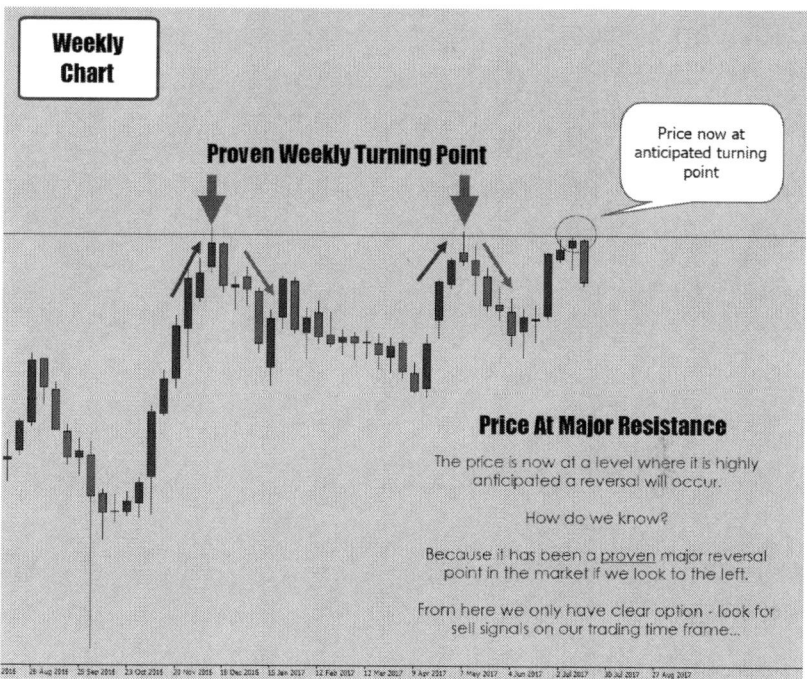

As you can see in the chart above, price are at a weekly resistance level, buyers were rejected twice from this level which indicates that the market is at a hot a point and it is likely to reverse.

What you can do as a price action trader is to switch to the daily time frame to look for a selling opportunity.

If you can find a price action setup near the weekly resistance level on the daily time frame, this is going to be a high probability setup to take into consideration.

See the example below:

THE CANDLESTICK TRADING BIBLE

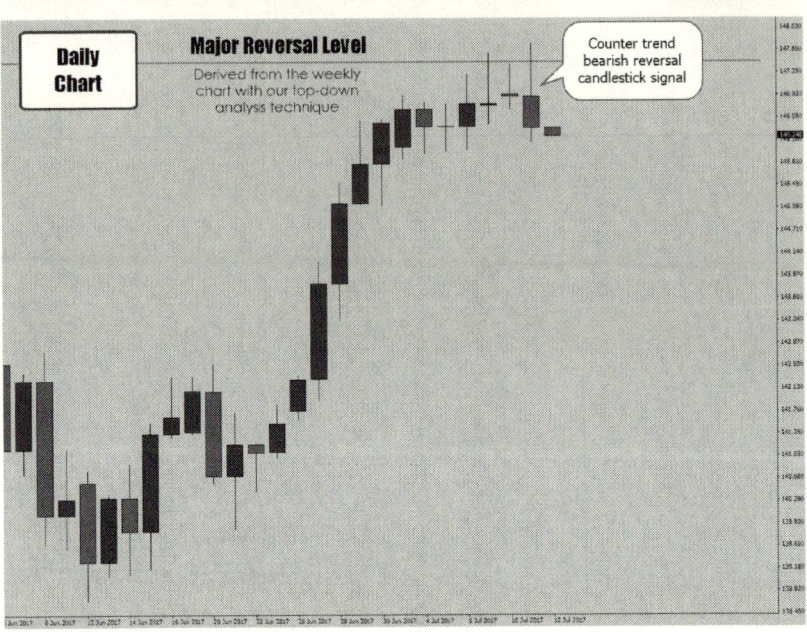

The daily chart above confirms our weekly analysis, as you can see; there is a clear bearish signal near the weekly resistance level.

The pin bar was rejected from that level, and there is also the formation of an inside bar false breakout.

This is a clear indication of a trend change.

See what happened next:

THE CANDLESTICK TRADING BIBLE

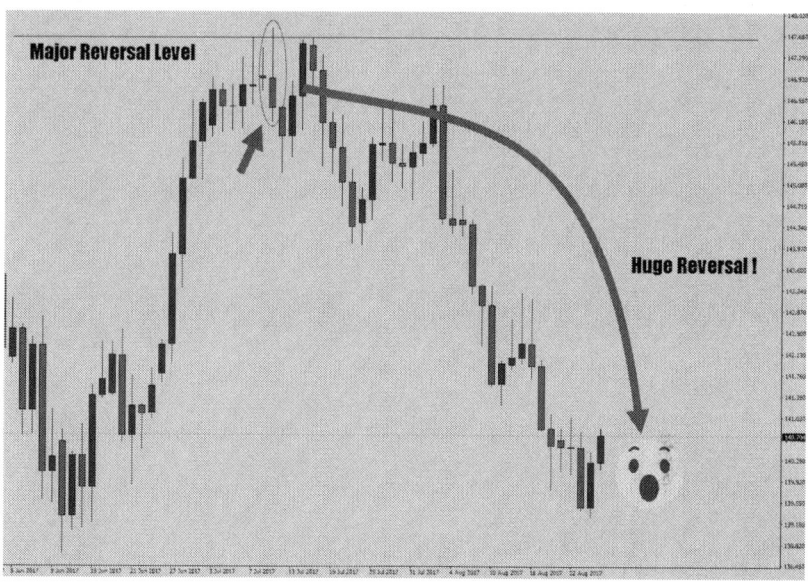

The example above shows that counter trend works if it is well mastered, it is a contrarian approach that requires experience, so if you are a beginner, i highly recommend you to stick with the trend, try to practice as much as you can the top down analysis concept with the trend, and when you master trading with the trend, you can then move to trade high probability counter trend setups.

There are many approaches used to time the market turns and plan trades, the most of these approaches lead to greater confusion and lack of confidence in the results.

Keeping the analysis simple is most often the best way to go, and top down analysis is one of the easiest approaches that i recommend to master if you want to trade the right way.

What you have to do right now is to open your charts and try to practice what you learnt in this chapter.

Try to identify the market trend using these techniques. It will be little confusing at the beginning, but with some screen time and practice, you will find it easy to identify the market direction.

Trading strategies and tactics

In the last chapters you learnt three important aspects of price action trading:

The first aspect is the market trends: you know how to identify the market trend using multiple time frames analysis. You know how to differentiate between trending markets, and range bounds markets. And you understand how each market moves.

The second aspect is the level: you learnt how to draw support and resistance, and how to draw trend lines, this skill will help you better enter the market in the right time.

The third aspect is the signals: you have seen different candlestick patterns, you understand the psychology behind its formation, and the message they send you.

These three aspects which are the trend, the level, and the signal are what we will use in our trading approach to make money trading any financial market.

I mean that when you open a chart, you will try to answer three important questions:

1-What the market is doing? Is it trending, consolidating, or is it a choppy market?

If it is trending, you know how to identify if it is an uptrend or a downtrend.

If it is a ranging market, you will see that it is trading horizontally between two boundaries. And if it is a choppy market, you close your chart and you stay away.

2-What are the most powerful levels in this market?

If the market is trending up or down, or it is ranging, you will try to find the most important support and resistance levels.

These levels are the best zones where you can buy and sell the market.

3-What is the best signal to enter the market?

The best signal to enter the market means the right time to execute your trade.

And this is what you will learn in the next chapter.

The pin bar candlestick pattern strategy

The pin bar candlestick is one of the most famous Japanese candlesticks; it is widely used by price action traders to determine reversal points in the market.

In this section, you will learn in detail how to identify potential pin bar signals, and the conditions needed for high probability setups.

A pin bar is a chart candlestick, it is characterized by a very long tail that shows rejection and indicates that the market will move in the opposite direction.

The area between the open and close is called the real body, typically all pin bars have a very small real body and a long shadow.

A Bullish pin bar is known for its lower wicks, and the bearish one is characterized by long upper wicks, the color of the candlestick is not quite important, however, bullish candles with white real body are more powerful than candles with a real black body.

On the other hand, a bearish pin bars with black real bodies are more important than the ones with white real bodies.

See how pin bars look like below:

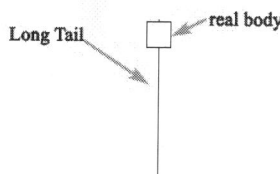

Bullish Pin Bar

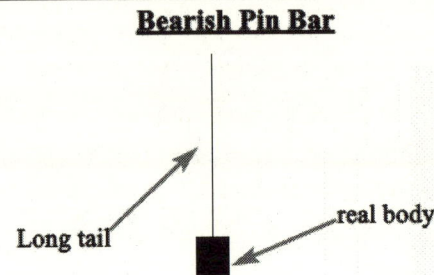

How to identify pin bar candlestick setups?

To be honest, quality price action setups don't exist in the market, because you will see that sometimes you can find a high probability

setup, you feel very excited about it and you take your trade with confidence, but at the end, you will be frustrated because the signal fails for unknown reasons.

That happens a couple of times, because the market doesn't move due to pin bar formations, what moves the market is the law of supply and demand.

Let me give you an example, if you identify a quality pin bar candle near a support key level in an uptrend market, this is a powerful buying signal to take, you shouldn't ignore it, but if the amount of money that buyers put in this trade is less than the amount of money that sellers risk in the same trade, the market will not go in your predicted direction.

If the signal fails, it doesn't mean that your analysis is wrong, or pin bars don't work, it is just because the market didn't validate your decision, therefore, you accept your loss, and you look for another opportunity.

You May ask yourself, why should we look for quality pin bar setups if the market doesn't respect them???

As you know, trading is a game of probabilities, there is no certainty, this is why you should evaluate your pin bar setups from multiple angles, and the fact that you are looking for quality setups means that you are trying to put the probabilities of success in your favor which is the right mindset of successful traders.

To determine whether or not a pin bar is worth trading, this price action signal should respect the following criteria:

-The pin bar formed in bigger time frames such as the 4 hour or daily time frame should be taken into consideration, because if you look at smaller time frames, you can easily spot lot of pin bar signals, these setups should be ignored, because smaller time frames generate lot of false signals. See the illustration below:

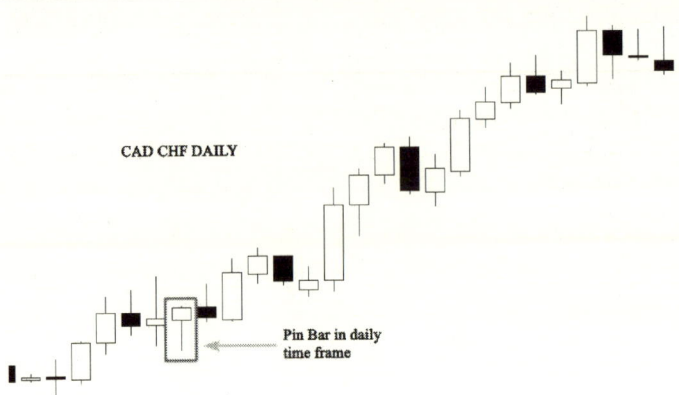

-The pin bar formed in line with the direction of the market is more powerful than the one which is formed against the trend.

- If you can identify a clear trend that means that you know who is in control of the market.

The formation of this candlestick pattern with the trend makes it so effective. See the chart below:

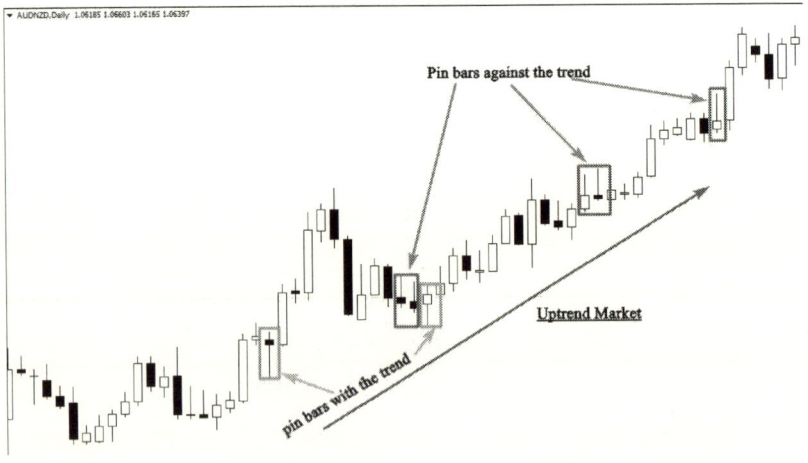

As you can see in the chart above, bullish pin bars that were formed in line with the uptrend work, and they should be taken into consideration.

But the bearish ones that were formed against the trend should be ignored.

-The anatomy of a pin bar is important as well, you have to make sure that the candlestick is a pin bar by looking at the distance between the real body and the tail.

Pin bars with longer tails are more powerful.

The Psychology behind the pin bar candle formation:

Pin bars are formed when prices are rejected, this rejection doesn't indicate a reversal signal, because this price action setup can form everywhere in your chart.

The most important areas to watch when trading pin bars are major key levels such as: support and resistance, supply and demand zones, and moving averages.

The formation of this candlestick chart pattern in these levels give a clear idea about what happens in the market.

If the rejection was near a support level for example, this is an obvious indication that the bulls are more powerful, and they are willing to push the market to go upward.

See the chart below:

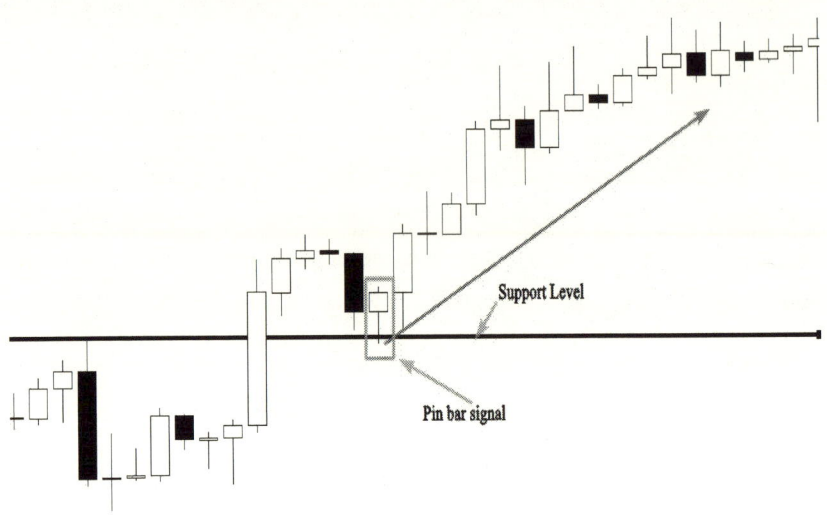

If the formation of this candlestick occurs near a resistance level, it indicates that the bears reject prices, and prevent the bulls from breaking this level. So, this means that sellers are willing to push the market downward. See the chart below:

If you understand the psychology behind this price action pattern formation, you will be able to predict what is likely to happen in the future, and you will make good trades based on high probability pin bar signals.

Trading the pin bar candlestick with the trend

If you are a beginner trader, i highly recommend you to stick with the trend, because pin bars that occur in trending markets offer good trading opportunities with high risk/reward ratio.

When you master trading it with the rend, you can then move to trade range-bounds markets or even counter-trends.

This strategy is simple, you start by identifying a clear uptrend or downtrend, and you wait for a pin bar to occur after a pullback to support or resistance level.

See the example below:

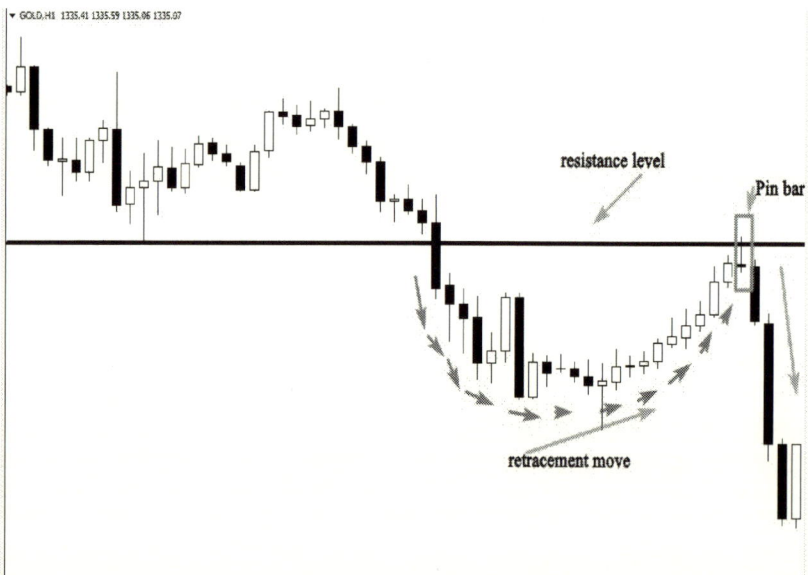

The figure below shows how this price action signal works if it is traded with the trend, as you can see, the price was rejected from the resistance level which indicates that the bears are still in charge of the downtrend.

The formation of the pin bar indicates the end of the retracement move, and the beginning of the impulsive move at the resistance level in line with the downtrend.

This is a high-quality setup because all the following criteria are respected:

1-The pin bar is well formed, and it is in line with the direction of the market.

2-The rejection occurred in a major key level which represents a hot point in the market (resistance level).

3-The risk to reward ratio is good, and it is worth trading.

Sometimes, even if the market is trending, we can't draw support and resistance levels, because prices move in a certain way which we can't spot static key levels.

If you are in this situation, you can use the 21-moving average which will act as a dynamic support in an uptrend market and a dynamic resistance in a downtrend market.

See the illustration below:

THE CANDLESTICK TRADING BIBLE

As you can see in the chart above, the market was trending down, using the 21 moving averages helps us to identify dynamic resistance levels, and high probability pin bar setups. See another chart below:

The 4-hour chart above illustrates how the 21-moving average could help us find key points in the market.

When prices approach the moving average, the buying pressure takes place in the market, and the price goes up.

The pin bar signal is clear on the chart, because the trend is bullish, the price action setup has a bullish anatomy as well, and the rejection from the 21-moving average is a confirmation signal to buy the market.

Trading tactics

When we identify the trend, (uptrend or downtrend) and the level (support or resistance).

And we find a pin bar near these levels in line with the direction of the trend. The second step is to know how to enter the market based on this candlestick pattern.

According to my experience, there are different entry options when it comes to trading pin bars; it all depends on the candle anatomy, the market conditions, and your money management strategy.

1-The aggressive entry option: this method consists of entering the market immediately after the pin bar closes without waiting for a confirmation.

This strategy will help you catch the move from the beginning, because sometimes the price goes higher after the close of the pin bar, and if you are not in the market, the trade will leave without you.

See the example below:

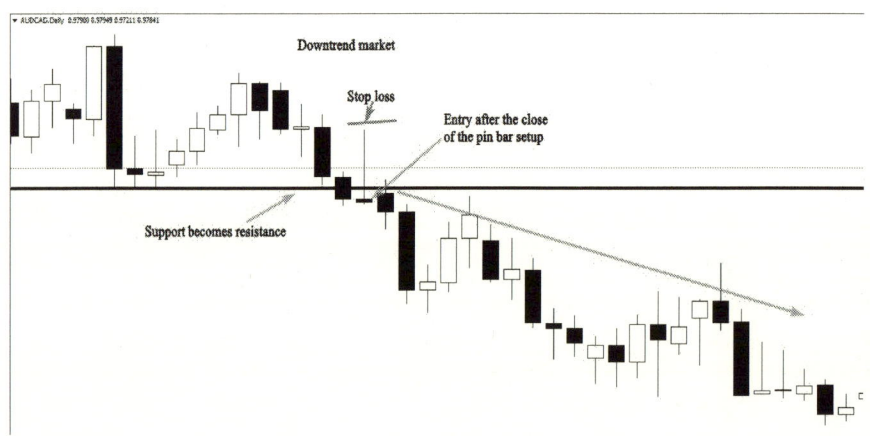

The chart above shows how an aggressive entry could help you to execute your trade in the right time without being left by the market.

And as you see, we took this trade because we had three important elements:

-The trend: The market was trending down, in this case we look for selling opportunities.

The level: In this chart we had a support level that becomes resistance.

The signal: A clear pin bar was formed after the retracement back to the resistance level.

When you have these three elements in the market, you just place your trade after the close of the pin bar, and your stop loss above the long tail. your profit target will be the next support level in case of a downtrend.

These three elements are quite enough for you to find high probability entries in the market.

The conservative entry option: this strategy consists of entering the market after 50% of the range bar retracement.

This strategy sometimes will work and it gives you more than 5:1 risk/reward ratio, and sometimes the market will leave without you. See the illustration below:

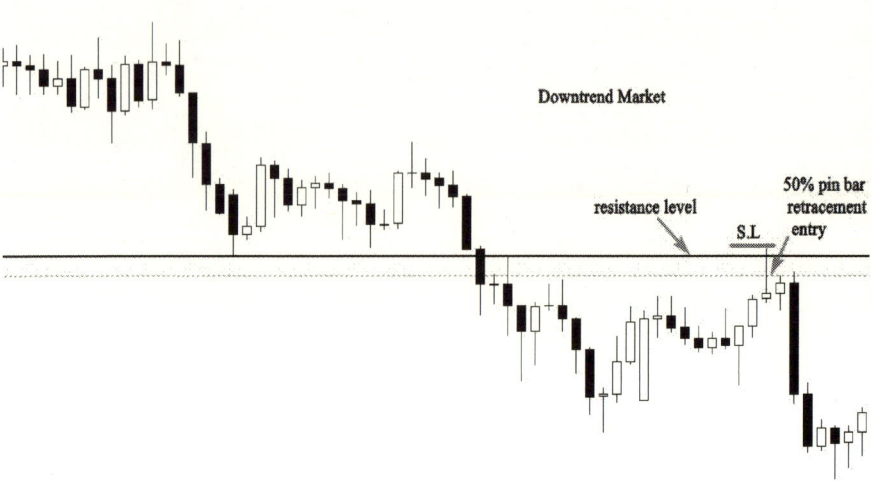

The illustration above gives us an idea about the power of conservative entries, as you can see, this entry method helps us decrease our risks and increase our rewards.

The trade above has more than 5:1 risk/reward ratio. One trade like this every month is quite enough to generate a decent income. See another chart below:

One of the drawbacks of this entry option is that the market sometimes doesn't retrace to 50% of the range bar, which will make you feel frustrated because the market will move to the profit target without you.

There is no wrong or right entry option, the both work great, but with screen time and experience, you will be able to decide whether to trade aggressively or conservatively.

Trading pin bars with confluence

Confluence happens when many technical indicators generate the same signal, this trading concept is used by price action traders to filter their entry points and spot high probability signals in the market.

It doesn't matter if you are beginner or advanced trader, trading with confluence is a must, because it will help you focus on quality setups rather than quantity, and it will enhance tremendously your trading performance.

Confluence means combination or conjunction, it is a situation in which two or more things join or come together, for example, if we are looking for a pin bar signal, we need to find other factors of confluence to confirm our entry; we are not going to take any pin bar that we find on our chart.

Factors of confluence:

The trend: it is one of the most important factor of confluence, this is the first thing that most successful traders look for on their charts, you can't trade any setup without identifying if it is in line with the direction of the market or not.

A bearish pin bar in a downtrend is more powerful signal than the one in a range-bound market.

Support and resistance levels and supply and demand areas: these major levels have a significant importance in the market, because all big participants watch these specific areas.

Moving averages: i personally use the 8 and 21 moving average, this technical trading tool acts as dynamic support and resistance, and it is a very important factor of confluence in trending markets.

Fibonacci retracement tool: I use the 61% and 50 % Fibonacci retracement to find the most powerful areas in the market.

Trend lines: drawing these lines on your charts give us an idea about the market direction and help us find the most important reversal points in the market.

When you are analyzing your chart, you are not obligated to find all these levels to determine whether the trade is valid or not.

If you can find just one or two factors of confluence that come up together with a good pin bar setup, this is quite enough to make a profitable trade.

For example: an obvious pin bar signal near support or resistance level in line with the direction of the market.

See the illustration below:

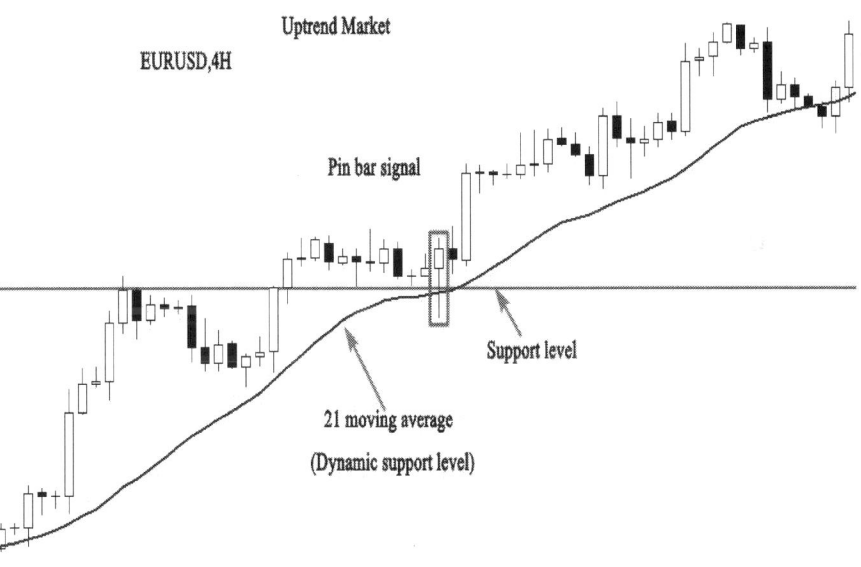

In the example above, we have a high probability setup with four factors of confluence.

1- **The Trend**: the market is trading up which means that we have to follow the trend and look for a buying opportunity.

2- **The level**: The support level is an important key level in the market. as you can see, price broke out of the resistance level that becomes support and pulled back to it.

3- **The signal**: The formation of **the bullish pin bar** after the retracement back to the resistance level that becomes support.

4- **Another signal**: The rejection of the pin bar from the support level, and the 21 moving average that acted as a dynamic support level.

All these factors work together to give us powerful trading signal to buy the market.

See another example:

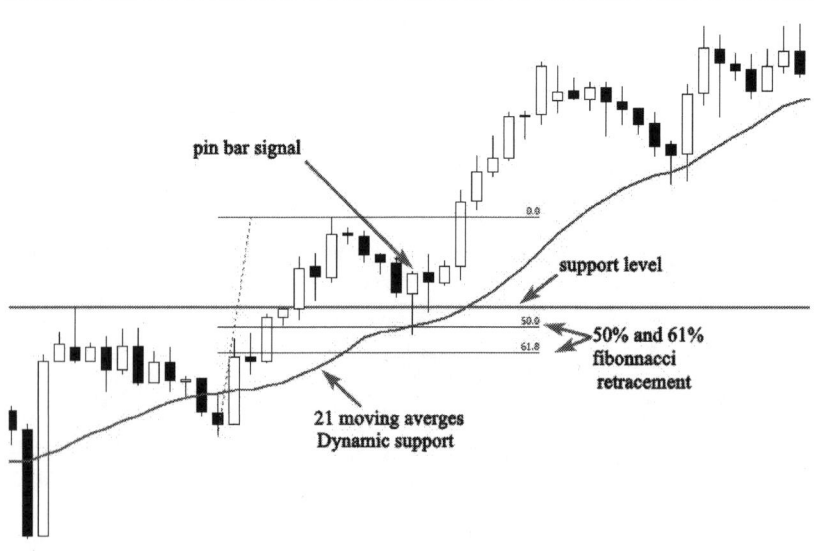

The example below shows 4 confluent levels that indicate a powerful trading signal, the first factor is the bullish trend, and the second one is the resistance level that becomes support.

The third one is the 21-moving average that acts as a dynamic support level. and the last factor is the pin bar formation near these levels in line with the bullish trend.

If you adopt this trading concept, you will completely change the way you perceive the market, and you will start trading like a sniper by waiting for the best trading setups to come to you, instead of trying hard to make trades happen.

Pin Bars trades examples

I will give you some trading examples to help you understand how to trade the pin bar candlestick pattern with the trend. and how to use the confluence concept to confirm your entries.

See the chart below:

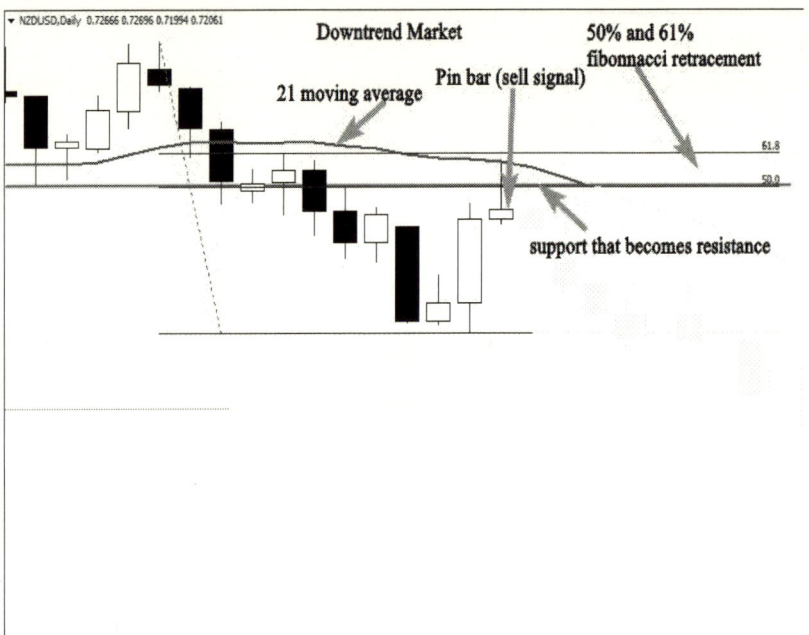

This is the NZDUSD daily chart, as you can see the market is trending down. this is the first information that we gather from this chart.

After the breakout of the support level that becomes resistance, the price retraced back to this level, and formed a pin bar candlestick pattern.

The formation of the pin bar near the resistance level indicates that the retracement move is over, and the beginning of an impulsive move is likely to happen.

When we put the 21 moving average and the Fibonacci retracement on the chart, we see that the pin bar is rejected from these levels which indicates that this level is very important and sellers are willing to push the market lower.

Here in this example we have solid reasons to sell the market, the first reason is the downtrend.

The second reason is the formation of the pin bar near the resistance level which indicates the end of the pullback and the beginning of a new move downward.

The third reason is the rejection of the pin bar from the resistance level, and from the 21-moving average,

The last reason is the pin bar rejection from the 50% Fibonacci retracement level which is considered to be one of the most powerful key levels in the market.

Look at the chart below to see what happened next:

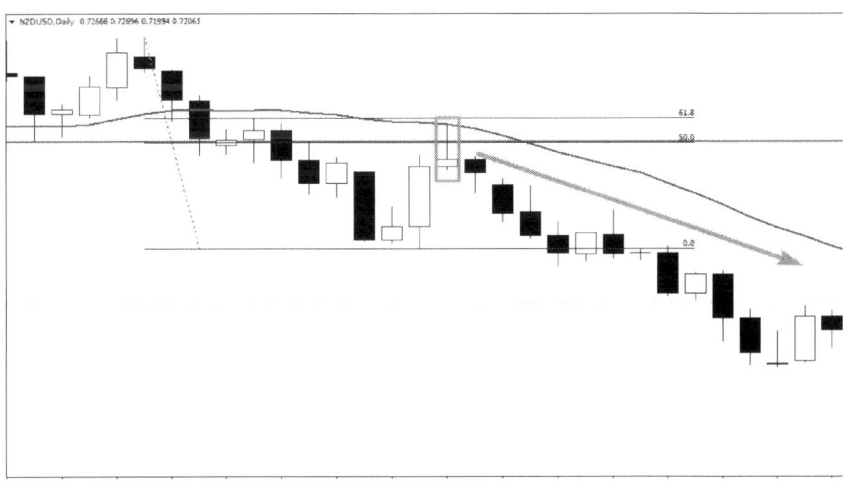

As you can see in the chart above, our analysis was right, because it was based on solid reasons to enter the market.

This is the method that i want you to learn to be able to trade the market successfully. Look at another chart below:

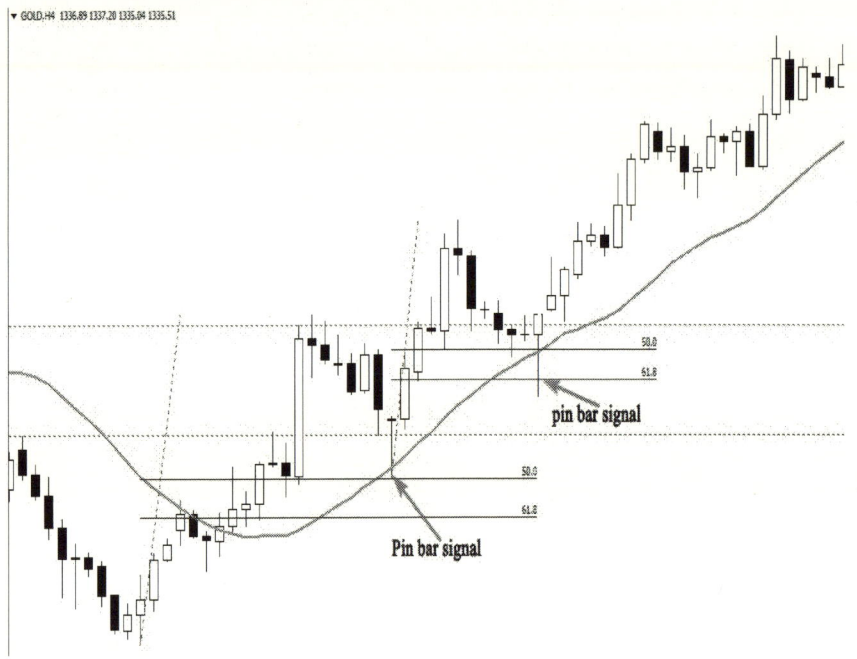

The chart above shows two important buying opportunities.

The market was trending up, the formation of the first pin bar after the retracement back to the support level was a high probability entry.

What confirms our entry is the rejection from the 21-moving average, and the 50% Fibonacci retracement.

The same thing happens with the second pin bar that allowed us to enter the market again and make more profits.

THE CANDLESTICK TRADING BIBLE

Trading pin bars in range-bound markets

We can say that a market is ranging when prices don't make any higher high and higher low and start trading horizontally between a definable level of support and a definable level of resistance.

Once i see that the market changes its behavior, i have to change my tactics and adopt a trading strategy that fits this new market condition.

To confirm a ranging market, i have to look for at least two touches of support level, and two touches of resistance level, and once i have identified the range, then it becomes very simple to trade it by going long when prices reaches the support level and going short when prices approach the resistance level.

See below an example of a range-bound market:

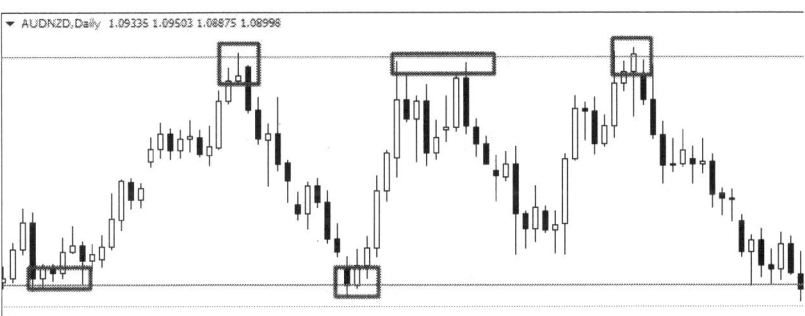

As you see, as prices approach the key support or resistance level, we have an opportunity to buy or sell the market; we need just to wait for a clear price action setup such as a pin bar candlestick.

Look at the illustration below:

103

THE CANDLESTICK TRADING BIBLE

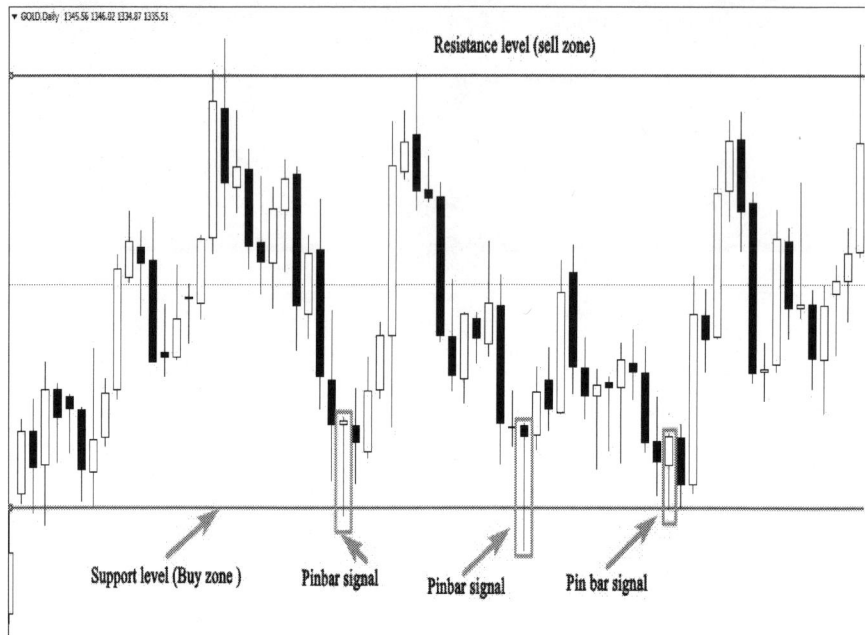

The illustration above shows us three trading opportunities, let me explain you how you can trade them successfully:

1-The first one is a pin bar rejected from the support level, you can place a buy order after the pin bar closes, or you wait for the market to touches the 50% of the pin bar range.

Your stop loss should be placed above the support level, and your profit target must be placed near the resistance level.

The risk reward of this trade is very attractive.

2-The second trading opportunity occurs near the support level, you place a buy order after the close of the pin bar, and your stop loss should be below the support level. your profit target is the next resistance level.

3-The third setup is an obvious buying opportunity; as you can see the market was rejected from the support level and formed a pin bar to inform us that buyers are still there, and the market is likely to bounce from the support level.

Trading from major key support and resistance levels is the easiest way to make money trading range-bounds markets, don't never try to trade any setup if it is not strongly rejected from these areas.

The second strategy is about trading in the direction of the breakouts of major key levels or waiting for the prices to retrace back to the breakout point and then you go long or you short the market.

See the example below:

The figure above illustrates a range-bound market, the price broke out of the support level and retraces back to the point of the breakout, and the formation of an obvious pin bar indicates a high probability signal to short the market.

This is how professional traders trade ranging markets based on this price action signal.

How to confirm pin bar signals using technical indicators

Using technical indicators to confirm your entries will increase your probability of the trade being profitable, i'am not telling you that you have to focus on indicators to generate signals, because this will never work for you, but if you can combine your price action strategies with the right indicators, you will be able to filter your signals and trade the best setups.

One of the best indicators that i use to confirm my entries when i examine a range-bound market is the Bollinger bands indicator.

This technical trading tool was developed by John Bollinger to measure a market's volatility.

The strategy is very simple, we will combine horizontal support and resistance with the upper and lower Bollinger bands false breakout, if prices are rejected from major key levels and from the bands, this is a confirmation that the market will bounce from these levels.

See an example below:

THE CANDLESTICK TRADING BIBLE

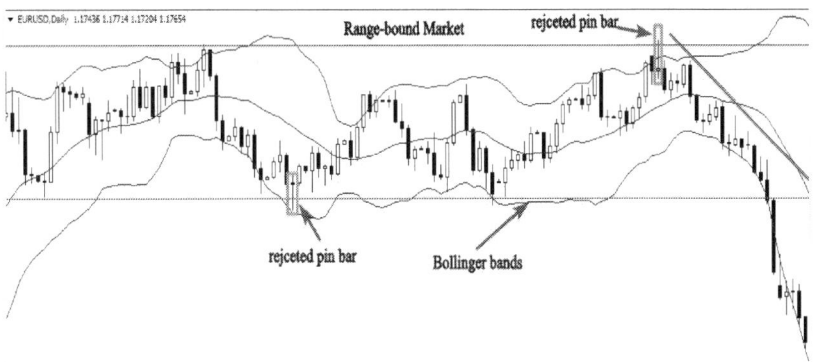

If you look at the chart above, you will notice how the Bollinger bands act as a dynamic support and resistance, when the market approaches the upper or the lower bands, prices bounce strongly.

So if we see that a pin bar is rejected from a horizontal key level and from bands, this is a clear confirmation to buy or sell the market.

This confirmation strategy is very simple, and it will help you decide whether to take a trade or ignore it, because trading is all about emotions, and sometimes, you will spot a nice pin bar signal in a range bound market, but you will find it difficult to make a decision.

What you have to do in this case is simple, just put your Bollinger bands on your chart, and if you see that the signal is rejected from horizontal levels and from the bands, don't over thinking about what you should do next.

Just execute your trade, place your stop loss and profit target then stay away and let the market do the work for you.

See another illustration below:

THE CANDLESTICK TRADING BIBLE

The daily chart above shows us how this indicator could help us execute our trades with confidence; the false breakout of the resistance level that was made by the pin bar was a powerful signal to short the market. The trade was confirmed by the false breakout of the upper band as well.

Remember that this technical indicator is used just as a confirmation tool in range-bound markets, don't use it to generate signals, use it always in combination with horizontal key levels, and you will see how this strategy will affect positively your trading account.

In conclusion, i recommend you to practice these strategies as much as you can before you open and fund your trading account.

The engulfing bar candlestick pattern

The engulfing bar pattern is one of the most powerful and profitable price action patterns, knowing how to use it properly as an entry signal will tremendously improve your trading profitability.

In this section you will learn how to use the engulfing bar pattern profitably, it doesn't matter if you are beginner or advanced trader, if you are looking for seriously a better trading strategy more than what you have been using. You have come to the right place.

What is an engulfing bar pattern?

This reversal candlestick pattern consists of two opposite colored bodies in which the second body engulfs or covers entirely the first one:

A bullish engulfing pattern forms at the end of a downtrend, it provides a clear signal that the buying pressure has overwhelmed the selling pressure.

In other words, the buyers are now involved.

A bearish engulfing pattern occurs at the end of an uptrend, it is a top trend reversal indicator, it shows that the bulls are no more in control of the market, and the price trend is likely to reverse.

See the illustrations below:

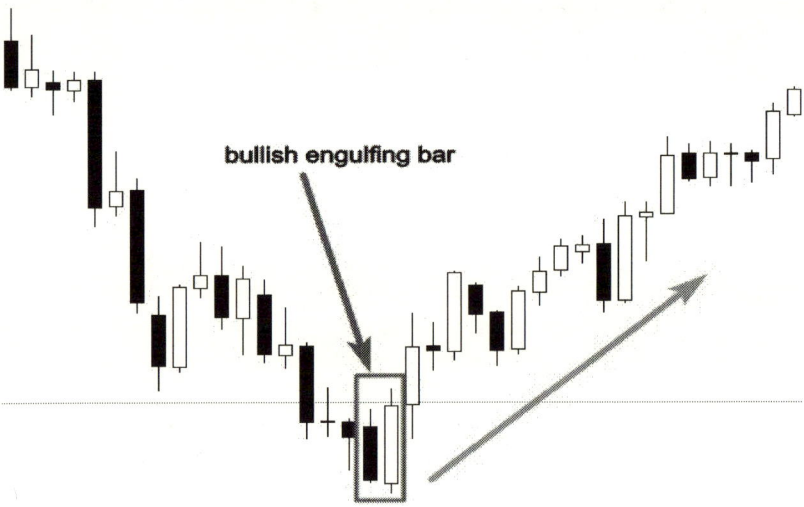

According to Steve Nison, the father of modern candlestick charting, this candle must meet three important criteria to be considered as a reversal pattern:

1-The market is in a clearly definable uptrend or downtrend

2-The engulfing candle comprises of two candlesticks, and the first body is entirely engulfed by the second one.

3- The second real body is the opposite of the first real body.

How to trade the engulfing bar price action signals?

To trade profitably this chart candlestick pattern, you need to respect three important elements:

1-The trend:

If you look at any chart, you will notice that there are times where the market is moving clearly in one direction, and times where it is moving sideways.

To be honest, trading the engulfing bar pattern with the trend is the easiest way to make money in the market.

You don't need to be highly knowledgeable about technical analysis to determine wither the market is trending or not.

Make it stupid simple, if the market is making series of higher highs and higher lows it is about an uptrend market, and if it is making series of lower highs and lower lows it is simply about a downtrend market.

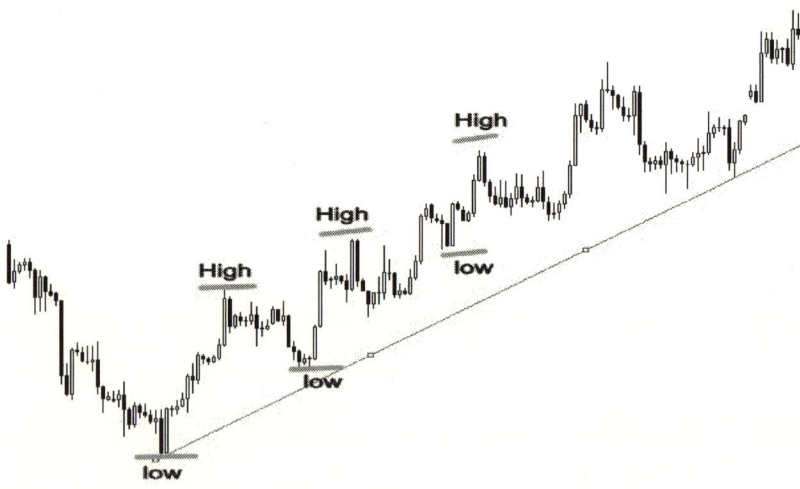

The illustration above shows a clear uptrend, you don't need to use an indicator to determine whether the market is trending or not, just look at your chart, and try to apply the concept of higher highs and higher lows and vice versa.

When you are analyzing your charts, bear in mind that the markets move in trends, and trading with the trend is the most important element in your technical analysis, there's no more important than the trend, don't never try to fight it, or to control it, otherwise you will pay expensively for trying.

You can't make money under any market conditions no matter how powerful is you're trading system, you have to be patient enough, and let the market tell you which direction is going to take.

Successful traders say, the trend is your friend, and if you want to master trading the engulfing bar pattern, your first rule is to follow the market direction, in other words, the trend should be your best friend.

2-The level:

When you find a clearly definable uptrend or downtrend, the next step is to identify the most important levels in the market. i mean the most powerful support and resistance.

If prices test a support level and stop, this is an indication that buyers are there, this area is watched by all participants in the market, because it represents a great buying opportunity.

Conversely, if prices test a resistance level and stop in an uptrend, this is a clear signal that selling strength is in the market.

The example below shows how the market participants interact with support and resistance levels:

THE CANDLESTICK TRADING BIBLE

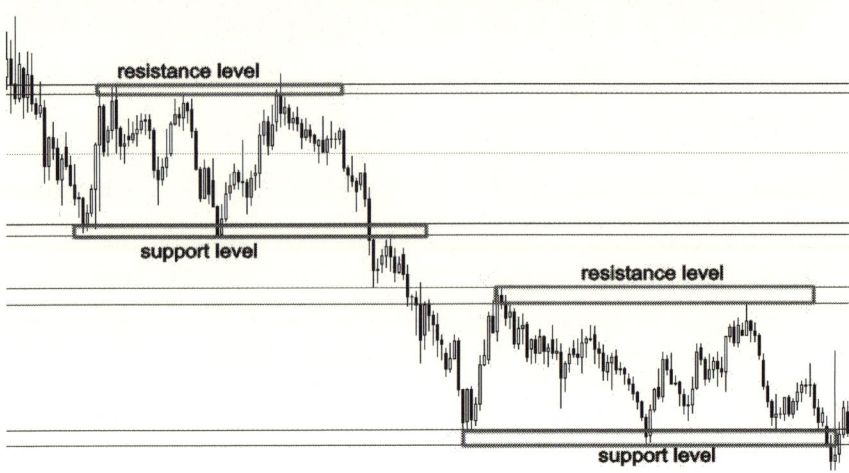

These levels take different forms such as: trend lines, channels, flags, triangles... and your ability to identify them in your chart will help you find better price levels in the market.

In trending markets, when prices pass through resistance level, that resistance could become support; see the illustration below to understand how to trade the engulfing bar pattern with support and resistance in a bullish or a bearish trend:

THE CANDLESTICK TRADING BIBLE

There are other technical tools that can help us find the best levels in the market such as: supply and demand areas, moving averages, and Fibonacci retracement ratios.

3-The signal:

The signal here is an engulfing bar pattern; you can apply the same rules when trading the inside bar candlestick pattern

Your ability to identify an engulfing candlestick at a key level in a clear uptrend or downtrend will greatly enhance the probabilities of making a wining trade.

See another example below:

Trading the engulfing bar with moving averages

Trading the engulfing bar pattern with moving averages provide a very profitable trading strategy, however, the lack of knowledge about using the moving average can damage dramatically your trading account.

Traders use moving averages in different ways:

-As a trend following tool to identify the direction of the trend, so they buy the market when prices are above 200 simple moving average. And they sell the market when it is below the 200 simple moving average

-To determine whether the market is overbought or oversold we just watch how prices interact with the moving averages, for example, in an uptrend, if prices move far from the moving averages, this is an indication that the market is overbought.

-To predict the trend, change by using the crossover strategy, if the moving average crosses over another, it is a signal of a trend reversal.

As any trading system, the moving averages have disadvantages; this is why you have to know how to use it successfully under the right market conditions.

This trading technical tool doesn't apply to all markets, don't never try to use it in range bound or untradeable markets.

Because you will get lot of false signals, and you will definitively blow up your trading account.

To the best of my knowledge, using the moving average as a dynamic support and resistance in trending markets, in combination with an engulfing bar pattern signal is the perfect way to make money in the market.

The strategy is very simple, we will use the 21 and the 8-simple moving averages in the daily and 4-hour time frames, we will define a clear bullish or bearish market and we simply buy when price pullbacks to the moving average and an engulfing bar pattern forms.

See the illustration below:

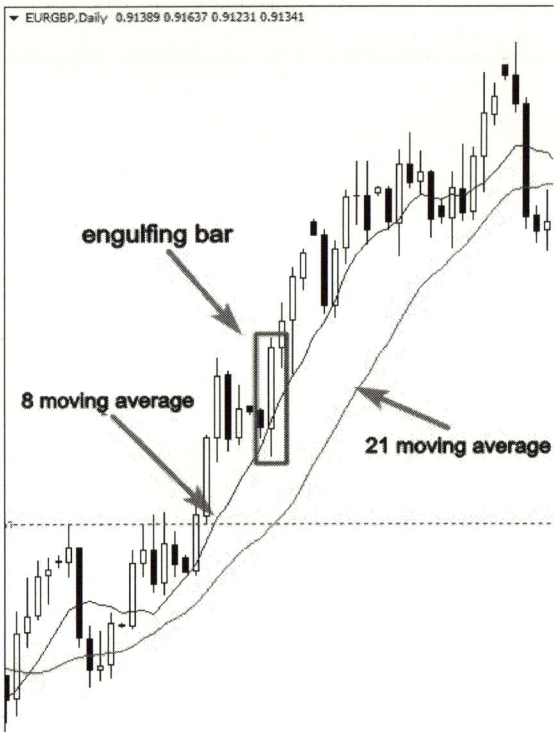

Conversely, if the moving average is trending down, it shows that the market is in a downtrend, we sell when price retrace to the moving average.

The screenshot below shows how prices interact with the moving average as dynamic resistance level, and how the engulfing bar pattern represented a high probability setup.

THE CANDLESTICK TRADING BIBLE

How to trade the engulfing bar with Fibonacci retracement

Traders use Fibonacci retracement in different ways, however, the most important Fibonacci retracement levels are the 50% and the 61% Fibonacci retracements, knowing how to use this tool in conjunction with Japanese candlestick will definitively maximize your profit potential.

According to chart technicians, the most major moves retrace around 50 % or 61 % Fibonacci retracement, this knowledge will provide you with the ability to predict with high accuracy the next major move in a trending market.

The strategy is very simple, you define a clear uptrend or downtrend, and then, you define major corrective levels by using Fibonacci retracement tool, if you see an engulfing bar pattern matches up with 50% or 61 % levels, it is a powerful price action trading signal like we see in the chart below:

In the example above, the engulfing bar price action signal matches up with the 50 % and 61 % Fibonacci retracement level, the resistance level that becomes support is another confirmation to take this high probability setup.

This trading strategy is very powerful, here is another example below that illustrates the power of 50% and 61 % Fibonacci retracement:

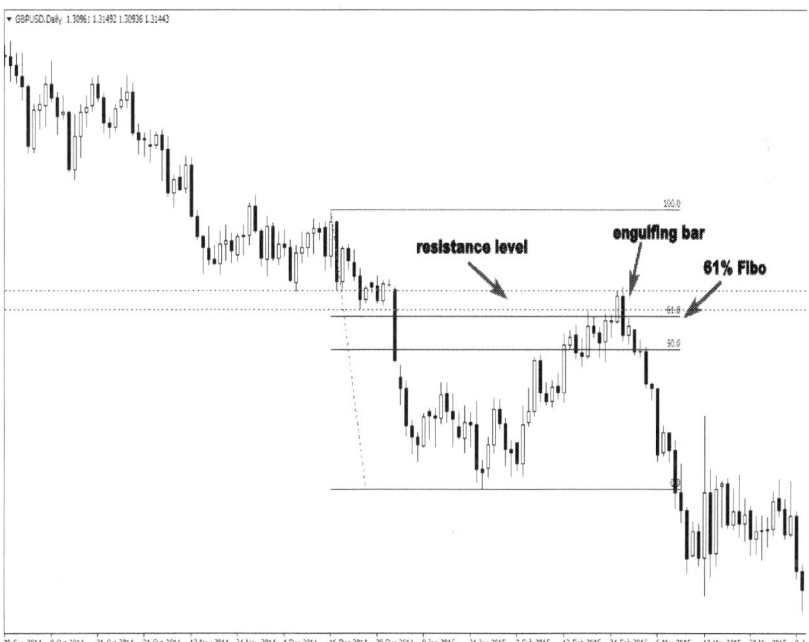

Trading the market from 50% and 61% Fibonacci levels means you are trading from better price levels, as a result, you will put as many probabilities in your favor as possible, and that will allow you to become one of the most successful traders.

Trading the engulfing bar with trendlines

Trend lines give traders an idea about the psychology of the market, especially, the psychology between buyers and sellers, moreover, it allows professional traders to determine whether the market is pessimistic or optimistic.

This technical trading tool is used in different ways, either as support and resistance by drawing them horizontally, or to identify price and time by drawing trend lines vertically. There is no wrong way in using trend lines.

In trending markets, we use simply trend lines to highlight a trend by connecting swing highs or swing lows in price; this way helps us find high probability entry setups in line with the general trend of the market.

See the illustration below:

By connecting the extreme highs, we had a trend line that acted as a resistance level and the formation of the engulfing bar pattern shows a good selling opportunity.

If you used just horizontal support and resistance levels, you will miss this profitable trade.

Learning about how to draw trend lines is never a bad idea, because it is the simplest analytic tool that you can use to analyze financial markets, it works in all markets, whether it's forex, commodities, futures, or options.

THE CANDLESTICK TRADING BIBLE

The chart above shows a bullish trend, the trend line acts as a support level, the price action signal that occurred created a great buying opportunity.

How to trade the engulfing bar in sideways markets?

One of the most difficult markets to predict can be the sideways and ranging markets, i always recommend traders to focus on trading trending markets, but the problem is that the markets spend more than 70 % of their time in ranging motion.

If you focus just on trending markets, you will probably leave lot of money on the table, this is the reason why learning how to approach range bound market is a must if you want to make decent living trading financial markets.

What is a range-bound market?

When the market stop making higher highs and higher lows in case of an uptrend or lower highs and lower lows in case of a downtrend, the price starts acting between specific high price and low price.

This is a clear signal that the market is ranging and no longer trending. See the illustration below:

As you see in the example above, the market is trendless, it is trading between horizontal support and resistance, and you can't apply the same techniques that you use in trending market to trade engulfing bar patterns in range bound markets.

Let me give you an example, when you are driving your car, you don't always drive the same way, if you are driving downtown, you try to drive slowly, because you know that driving fast can put your life or other's life in danger

But when you are driving in a highway, you're driving style changes completely, because you know that you can drive fast. So, you always try to adapt your driving style to the appropriate situation.

You have to do the same thing when you are trading the engulfing bar pattern, because all price action strategies we discussed before will not work in range bound markets, and you have to use the right techniques that fit these market conditions.

Before talking about the right way to trade trendless markets, you have to be selective about trading range bound markets to protect your trading account, because not all sideways markets are worth trading. You have to know how to differentiate between sideways and choppy markets.

See the illustration below about choppy markets:

As it is illustrated above, the market trades in a crazy way, we can't identify major support levels and resistance. You have to stay away from these types of markets, otherwise, you will definitively damage your trading account.

Trading the engulfing bar candle in range bound market is very simple, the first strategy is going to be about trading this price action pattern from major support and resistance levels like we see below:

The second strategy is to trade the breakout of the range or to wait for the pullback. See the illustration below :

The third strategy is to trade the false breakout of the major support or resistance level.

128

False breakouts are one of the most powerful price action strategies, it occurs in all types of markets, and if you know how to use it in combination with the engulfing bar pattern in a major support level or resistance, you will make money in the market, because you will buy intelligently the bottoms and sell the tops.

See the illustration below:

Trading the engulfing bar with supply and demand zones?

Supply and demand areas are more powerful than support and resistance, it is the place where banks and institutions are buying and selling in the market, if you can identify these turning points, you will make a difference in your trading account.

To trade the engulfing bar pattern successfully with supply and demand areas, you have to be able to identify quality supply and demand levels on a chart, according to my experience; there are three factors that define quality supply and demand areas:

1-The strength of the move:

Pay more attention to the way the price leaves the zone, if the market leaves the area quickly, this is an indication that banks and institutions are there.

2-Good profit zone:

You have to make sure that the level provides a good risk/reward.

3-Bigger time frames:

The daily and 4-hour supply and demand areas are the most powerful zones in the market.

The chart below shows a quality supply area, as you can see the move was very strong, and that indicates that banks and institutions were there.

The formation of an engulfing bar was a clear signal that the bears are still willing to sell from the same price level.

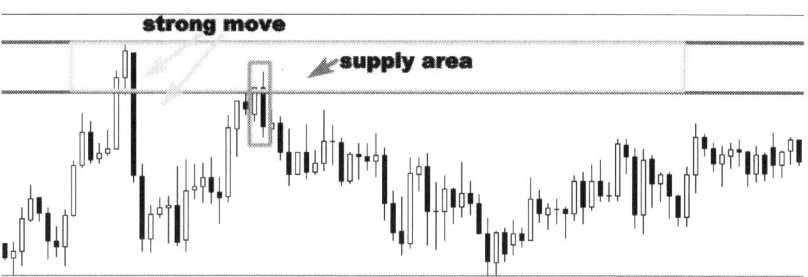

See another example of these areas:

I think that it's not complicated to identify these zones, because they are characterized by strong moves. The secret behind supply and demand areas is that big players put their pending orders there, when the market approaches these zones, we see a crazy move from these levels.

If you can combine trading supply and demand areas with the engulfing bar price action signal, you will increase your chances to make money as a trader.

Money management trading rules

So far you have learnt how to identify high probability setups in the market; this doesn't mean that all engulfing bar patterns are worth trading.

Price action signals with low risk /reward ratios should be ignored.

Once the criteria for a high probability setup are in place, there is no more analysis to be made, just make sure your trade has a potential of 2:1 risk to reward ratio.

I mean that the amount of money you will win has to be twice the amount of money you will risk or more.

See an example below:

As you can see all the conditions were in place to take a buying order, the market was ranging, as we discussed before, major demand and supply zones are the best price levels in sideways markets.

The formation of an engulfing bar in the demand area is a good trading opportunity, but you have to look at the risk /reward to make sure that the trade respects your money management's rules.

This trade has 3:1 risk to reward which increases your chances to be winner in the long term, because if you risk 200 dollars in this trade, you are likely to win 600 dollars. It is very important to calculate your risk to reward ratio before taking any single trade.

Case study

Imagine you take 10 trades with 3:1 risk /reward on each single trade, I mean when you win you get 600 dollars, and when the market goes against you, you lose 200 dollars.

Let's suppose you lost 7 trades and you won just 3 trades. Let's do the math to know if you are winner or loser.

Seven losing trades will cost you 1400 dollars, and 3 wining trades will make you 1800 dollars.

As you see you lost seven trades, but you are still making money. This is the magic of money management.

The entry and exit strategy

Don't try to be smarter than the rest of traders, keep it simple, you know what you are looking for, when you identify an engulfing bar pattern, and you think all conditions are in place to execute your trade. Take an order immediately after the price action signal forms, put your stop loss below the candlestick pattern, and look at simply the chart to find the next support or resistance level, this is going to be your profit target.

See the illustration below:

THE CANDLESTICK TRADING BIBLE

When you set your protective stop and your target, don't never look back, let the market tell you if you are wrong or right. This will help you trade successfully out of your emotions.

If the market goes against you, you will not feel good, it's normal, losing money can be emotionally painful, it is our human nature, nobody wants to lose, especially when it is about money, in the trading environment, you have to think differently, and accept the fact that losing is a part of the game.

Studies have shown that successful traders don't risk more than 2% of their equity on each single trade.

If you are beginner, don't risk more than 1%. Don't risk money you can't afford on a single trade even if the engulfing bar pattern you identify indicates a high probability signal.

THE CANDLESTICK TRADING BIBLE

No matter how smart you are, you have to think always in term of probabilities, bear in mind that you can experience series of losing trades, and if you risk too much money, you will not survive longer.

The inside bar candlestick pattern

The inside bar candlestick pattern is one of the most powerful chart setup that professional traders look out; however, most traders fail to trade it successfully.

Lack of skills and knowledge and poor education are the major reasons why most price action traders don't make money trading this Japanese candlestick.

What is an inside bar candlestick pattern?

An inside bar is two candlesticks, the first one is called the mother candle, it is big and large, and the second one is smaller and it is located inside of the mother bar.

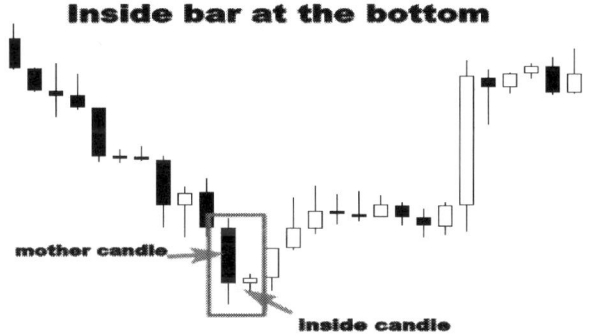

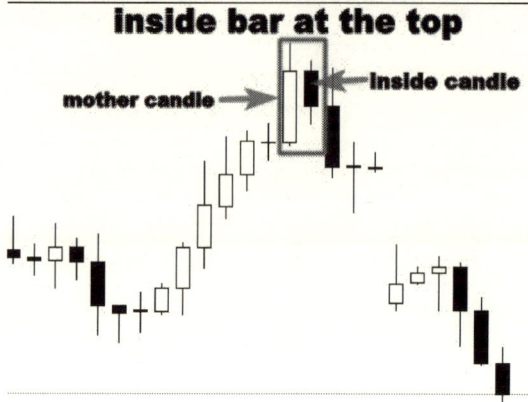

The illustration above shows inside bars at tops and at bottoms, as you can see, the second small bar is completely contained by the first one which is the opposite of the engulfing bar pattern.

The inside bar is seen as a reversal pattern, because it indicates that the market trend is likely to change especially when it is located at tops or bottoms.

It is also considered as a continuation signal in strong trending markets.

According to Thomas Bulkowski, a successful investor, and trader with over thirty years of market experience:

A bearish inside bar pattern in a bull market can indicates a bearish reversal in about 65% of the time.

And in a bull market, it represents a bullish continuation signal in about 52% of the time.

And a bullish abandoned baby as he call it, is considered a bullish reversal pattern 70% of the time in bull markets, and 55% in bear markets

The psychology behind the pattern formation

The inside bar formation indicates a period of consolidation, in case of a bullish trend, it reflects that the bulls are not buying any further on the second day, it is represented by a small black candle on the second day, after a strong uptrend.

And in case of a bearish trend, it means that sellers are not in control of the market any more, it is reflected by a small white candle after a strong downtrend.

Your understanding of the psychology behind this pattern will help you better identify major turning points in the market, and time correctly your entry and exit.

How to trade the inside bar candlestick patterns?

The inside bar can be traded successfully in trending markets particularly if the market is moving strongly.

Because the formation of this price pattern provides you with a great opportunity to join the big move.

This strategy is very simple, you have to identify a strong trend, and wait for the formation of an inside bar pattern in line with the direction of the market.

The formation of this pattern indicates that the market pauses before making its next move; this will allow you to enter the market in the right time and make big profits.

See the illustration below to learn more:

THE CANDLESTICK TRADING BIBLE

Trading inside bars in trending markets

As it is illustrated above, the market is trending down; the formation of inside bar patterns gave us three opportunities to join the trend.

If you are used to our trading approach, you will only look for selling opportunities, this way, you are not fighting big institutions and central banks, you are just trading in the direction that is favored by the market.

You can place a sell order after the breakout of the pattern as it is mentioned in the chart above, and your stop loss order should be placed above the mother candle. Your profit target is the next support level.

See another example below:

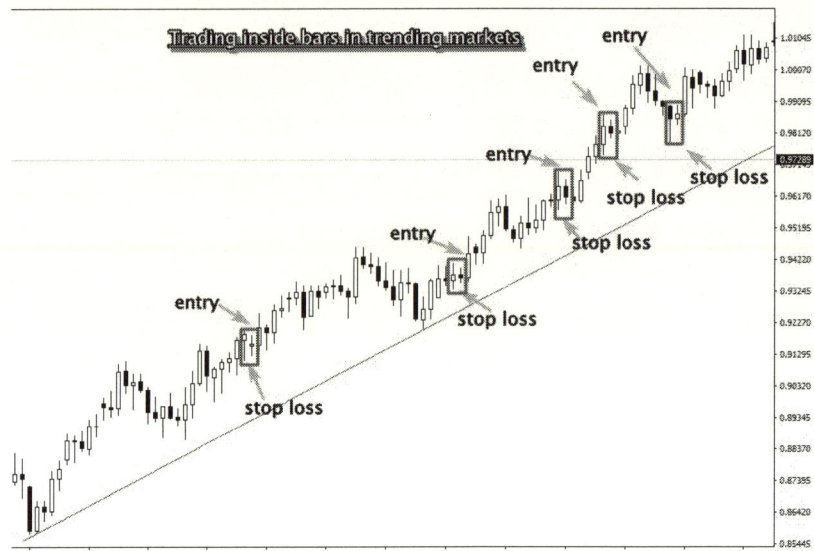

From the above chart, we can see how this price action setup work significantly as a continuation pattern, to be honest, you are not going to take all these signals into considerations.

You have to look for significant patterns that form in specific areas in the market such as support and resistance, Fibonacci retracement levels, moving averages, or pivot points.

Don't worry about that, because we will learn about the important trading tools that we will need to use in combination with inside bar setups to make the best trading decisions

How to trade the inside bar breakout with support and resistance

Technical analysis can be very complicated if you don't focus on the most important basics, such as support and resistance levels.

These areas represent a psychological level where the game is played between buyers and sellers, let me give you an example:

If sellers overcome buyers they will push the price below the support level. Some buyers will feel afraid to lose money, because they see that the support level is broken .so, they will get out, and sell the market again to cover their loss.

Other participants will notice that sellers are in control of the market, they will decide to sell the market and help the bears push the price to go down.

As a trader, if you have enough knowledge about support and resistance levels, when you open your chart, you will notice that the support level is broken, and the bears are in control of the market, this is a good selling opportunity right? But the question is, what is the right time to enter the market?

The inside bar pattern is one of the most reliable price action signal that will give you the right time to enter the market and make big profits.

Once you understand how to use it in combination with these levels, you will get clearly what the market is telling you, and you will make good trading decisions.

See the chart below:

THE CANDLESTICK TRADING BIBLE

The illustration below shows how sellers broke the support level, the formation of the inside bar pattern after the breakout of this level signals indecision in the market.

Right now, no one knows if the support level is really broken, if you sell at market immediately after the breakout of this level, you are making an aggressive entry, which is little tricky and dangerous, because the breakout is not confirmed.

But if you are used with trading inside bars and you understand the psychology behind their formations, you will know that the safest entry should be after the breakout of this pattern.

The breakout of this candlestick pattern is a clear confirmation that the market is not still in an indecision period, and sellers are obviously in control of the market. See another example.

THE CANDLESTICK TRADING BIBLE

The chart above shows how the market participants interact with these levels, and how the resistance level acts as barrier.

The market has had difficulty rising above; this horizontal level prevents buyers twice from rising any further. But in the third attempt, buyers broke through the resistance level.

What is interesting is what happened after the breakout, look at the chart again, you will notice that there is a clear inside bar pattern formed over there.

The formation of this price action pattern indicates that the breakout is not yet confirmed, remember, an inside bar formation means indecision and hesitation. So, you have to be careful, and bear in mind that a false breakout scenario is possible.

What will make a difference between you and other traders is your deep understanding of how this pattern works, in this chart above, you will know that the best time to place a buy order should be after the breakout of the inside bar pattern not after the breakout of the horizontal level.

THE CANDLESTICK TRADING BIBLE

Tips on trading the inside bar price action setups

1-Trade the bigger time frames

I'm not against trading lower time frames, you can trade this setup on 5 minutes time frame using other technical indicators to filter your signals and take just high probability setups.

But you have to be an experienced trader, if you are beginner

i recommend you to stick with trading this signal in bigger time frames such the daily and the 4-hour time frame.

Trading this setup on lower time frame will increase your chance to overtrade the market and take low probability price action signals. And this is the quickest way to blow up your trading account.

If you focus just on bigger time frames, this will allow you to set and forget your trade instead of being emotionally controlled by the market.

2- Trade the dominant trend

You should start trading inside bars in line with the direction of the market, especially in a strong bullish or bearish trend, but don't never try to trade it against the trend if you are a newbie.

When you feel like you master trading this pattern with the trend, you can move to trade range bound markets, and counter trends.

3- Trade only from key levels

Remember that not all inside bars are worth your hard-earned money; there are specific locations where this setup works great, so make sure that your signal is located in a key level in the market.

4- Find different factors of confluence

Trading with confluence means combining different signals to make the best trading decision.

To trade using this concept you need to look for a point in the market where two or more levels are coming together and wait for an obvious signal to form.

This trading method will give you confidence in your trading approach and it will allow you to avoid over-trading.

How to trade the false breakout of the inside bar candlestick pattern?

Have you ever placed an order with confidence thinking that the market is going to go up, but price hints your stop loss before it starts turning out to your predicted direction?? I have been a victim of stop hunting, and i was very disappointed, but that happens several times in the market.

Banks and financial institutions know how we trade the market, they know how we think, and where we put our stop losses and profit targets, this is the reason why they could easily take money from us.

One of the most famous strategies that big players use to take money from novice traders is called stop loss hunting strategy.

This strategy consists of driving prices to a certain level where there are massive stop loss orders, and the purpose is to create liquidity, because without liquidity, the market will not move.

Once stop losses are hunt, the market goes strongly in the predicted direction.

The interaction between big participants and novice traders create repetitive patterns in the market, one of the most important candlestick pattern that illustrates how big financial institutions manipulate the market is **the inside bar false breakout pattern.**

Your understanding of this repetitive setup and your ability to detect it on your charts will help you better exploit it to make money instead of being a victim of market makers and banks manipulations.

This price action signal is formed when price breaks out from the inside bar pattern and then quickly reverses to close within the range of the mother bar.

See the illustration below:

Bearish inside bar false breakout

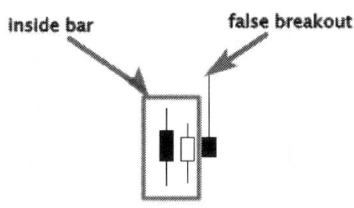

Bullish inside bar false breakout

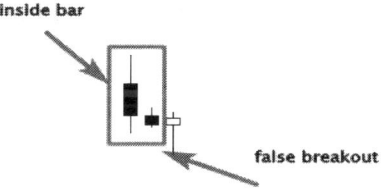

As you can see, there are two types of this price action pattern:

A bullish inside bar false breakout that forms when the market is trending down and it is also considered as a bullish reversal signal when it is formed near a key support or resistance level.

A bearish inside bar false breakout that occurs in a bullish trend and it is seen as a bearish reversal pattern when it is found near an important level in the market.

This setup can be considered as a continuation pattern if it is traded with the trend.

Inside Bars false breakouts trading examples

In my own experience, the most important levels that traders should look for to trade this signal are the following:

-Support and resistance levels, and supply and demand areas

-Fibonacci retracement levels, particularly, the 50% and 61% retracement levels.

-21 moving averages and trend lines in trending markets

-Horizontal levels in range-bound markets

Here is an example of how to trade inside bar false breakout in a trending market:

As you see in the chart above, the market was trending down, that indicates that sellers are in control of the market, so if you decide to sell the market near the resistance level, all probabilities will be in your favor.

But the question is when to enter the market? And where to put my stop loss?

If you enter the market aggressively before the breakout of the mother candle, and you put your stop loss above it, the market will take your stop loss and go in the predicted direction.

See the illustration below:

As illustrated above, big players hunt novice traders stops before pushing the market to go down, if your stop loss was near the resistance level, you would be out as well, if you don't understand the reason why, it is simply because you were a victim of big players hunting stop strategy.

If you are familiar with trading the inside bar false breakout, you will understand what happened in the market, and you will simply take advantage of this manipulation instead of being trapped by the market. See the example below:

As it is illustrated above, the inside bar false breakout gave us a good selling opportunity.

If you are able to identify this setup, and you understand the psychology behind it, there should be no reason not to get into the position.

THE CANDLESTICK TRADING BIBLE

Trading inside bar false breakouts with Fibonacci retracements

I don't really know if you are familiar with this technical trading tool, however, I will try to show you how to use it in a simple and efficient way in combination with the inside bar false breakout.

What you have to know is that in an uptrend or a downtrend, the market creates impulsive moves and pullbacks.

The Fibonacci retracement helps us highlight the most important pullbacks levels in the market.

The best Fibonacci retracement levels that i personally use are the 50% and 61% levels, according to my experience these levels are the most important areas that experienced trader watch in their charts.

Our strategy is simple, we select the technical tool on our chart, and if the market moves strongly, we wait for retracements, if the pullback reaches 50% or 61 % levels, we need just a price action signal to confirm our entry. See the example below:

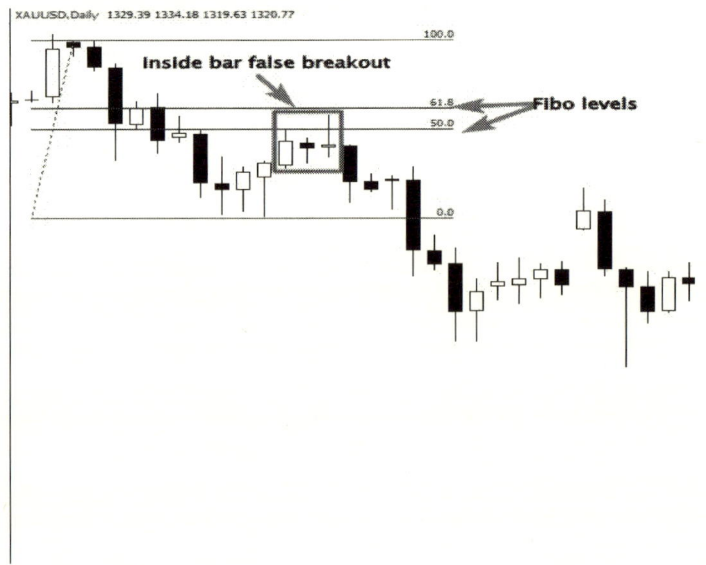

THE CANDLESTICK TRADING BIBLE

By adding this technical trading tool to your strategy, you will be able to identify potential trade set-ups in the market, if you analyzed the chart above without using it, you wouldn't know the reason why the market dropped after the pullback.

Fibonacci tool can be used to trade the pin bar, the inside bar and the engulfing bar setup as it was discussed in pervious sections.

The trade above is very profitable because there are lots of factors of confluence that encourage us to place a sell order.

The first reason is the trend, it is obviously down, the second reason is the key Fibonacci ratios that represent a resistance level, and the third one is the inside bar false breakout.

One signal is not quite enough to make a good trading decision, you have to look for multiple triggers that support your analysis, this way, you will put the odds of success in your favor.

Look at another potential trade below:

As you can see, the price moved higher, pulled back to reach our key ratios, and then continue higher. The formation of the inside bar false breakout in this area indicates that the pullback has finished and another strong move will take place.

Understanding the market structure is very important to know how to use this strategy in your advantage, if the market is trending, you can trade the inside bar false breakout as we discussed before.

But if the market is ranging, you have to change your tactic.

See the illustration below:

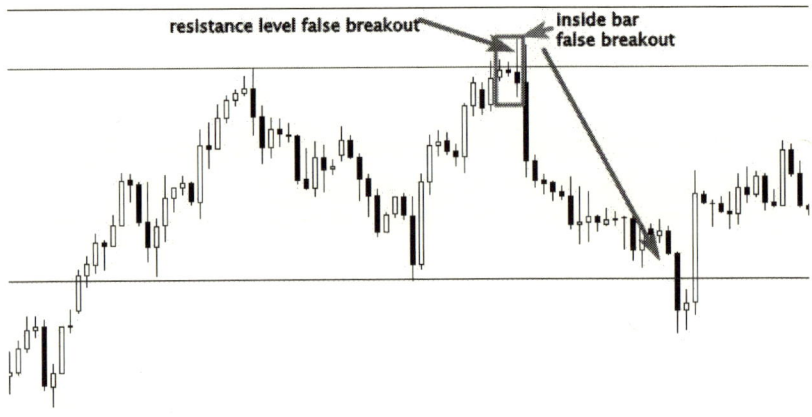

In the chart above, the market is trading between horizontal support and resistance levels, as you see if you had entered as soon as the market breaks out from the inside bar and the resistance level, you will be caught in a false breakout.

The false breakout has formed because amateurs tried to predict the breakout of the inside bar and the horizontal level early to pick the top, but the market fake them out and formed a bull trap.

If you find this pattern in your chart, and you understand that buyers were trapped by sellers, take this trade without hesitation, because it is very profitable and it has a good risk/reward.

You place a selling order after the close of the break bar, and you set your stop loss above it, your profit target is the next support level.

This strategy is not complicated, but it requires time and practice to master it, bear in mind that a false breakout doesn't happen every time, and not all false breakouts are worth trading.

The benefits of trading the false breakout of the inside bar candlestick pattern:

If you master trading this pattern, this will allow to stay away from trapped traders and enter the market when novice traders have to get out with a loss.

This strategy is not a holy grail, you have to be prepared to accept some losing trades, but what is interesting about it, is that the risk reward of this signal has a great potential, because when big participants surprises amateurs and take their money, the market moves very strongly, and if you can analyze correctly what happened, you will enter in the right time and make big profits. Imagine risking say 50 points for 400 points profits.

Using this price action strategy will help you predict proper turning points in the market in advance and understand how banks and financial institutions trade the market.

Trades Examples

In this section, i will show you different trades examples to help you understand how to trade the market using all the strategies discussed in the previous sections. See the first example below:

As you can see in the chart above, the market is trending down, so as a price action trader, i will try to follow the trend and look for powerful signals at the most powerful key levels.

The first signal we got is a pin bar that was rejected from a support level that becomes resistance.

The second factor that support our decision to sell the market is the rejection of the pin from the 50% Fibonacci retracement.

The third factor that encourages us to take this signal is the rejection of the pin bar from the 21 moving average that was acting as a dynamic resistance level.

The second signal was an engulfing bar candlestick pattern, as you can see in the chart, this candlestick pattern was formed at a resistance level in line with the direction of the market.

This is how you can trade trending markets using our price action signals. It's simple just identify the trend, and the key levels, it can be a support or resistance level, a 21 moving averages, or 50% and 61% Fibonacci retracement.

Wait for a pin bar, an engulfing bar, an inside bar, or an inside bar false breakout to form near these levels in line with the direction of the market, and then execute your trade. It's not complicated.

See another example below:

As you can see in the chart above the market is trading horizontally between the support and the resistance level.

This market is completely different from trending markets, and the strategy to trade it must different as well.

In ranging markets, we trade from the boundaries, i mean from support and resistance levels, don't never try to trade inside the range.

In the chart above, we had two powerful signals, the first signal was a pin bar that was strongly rejected from the resistance level, and the second signal was an inside bar formed near the support level.

See another chart below:

As you can see in the chart above, there are three powerful pin bar signals. When the market approaches the 21 moving average that acts as a resistance level, sellers reject buyers, and form a pin bar that gives us a good entry point.

Money management strategies

Now you have the strategies, you know how to analyze the market, you know when to buy, when to sell, and when to exit, you know also when to stay away from the market.

This is important for you as a trader to know, but you are still missing the key to the castle. The money management plan.

The most important thing that traders don't talk about is the money management. This is what makes a difference between successful traders and losers.

If you trade without a money management plan, you are just wasting your time and money. Because nothing is going to work for you, even if you have the most powerful trading system in the world.

Most traders focus on how to enter the market, they spend months and years looking for the right system. i don't want you to think like them, you should think differently if you want to become a successful trader.

Money management: Position sizing

One of the most important component of money management is position sizing, what i mean by position sizing is the number of lots you are risking per trade.

All forex brokers now offer mini lots as the default position size. The smallest value for a mini lot is approximately 1$.

There are forex brokers that offer 10 cents for a mini lot which represent an opportunity for traders who don't have bigger accounts, they can begin with 250$, and they still have chance to grow it.

When it comes to position sizing, you should think in terms of dollars instead of pips. Let's say you are trading 3 mini lots of CAD/USA, this means you bought or sold 30.000 worth of us dollars.

If the market moves in your favor, you will win an amount of money equal to 3$ per pip. If you make 20 pips, you would have profited 60$.

Let's break it down, 1standard lot is worth about 10$ per pip. And 1mini lot is worth about 1$ per pip, and 1 micro lot is equal to 10 cents.

If you open a mini trading account, you should think in term of the dollars risked instead of pips.

Let's say you put 50 pips stop loss and 100 pips as a profit target. This means that if the market hits your stop loss you will lose 50 pips which is 50$, and if the market hit the profit target, you will win 100$.

The size of your position depends on whether you have a standard or a mini account, and how many lots you are trading. This information is important to you because this will help you know how much money you risk on each trade.

The risk to reward ratio

The risk to reward ratio concept is what will make you a winner in the long run. Before you enter any trade, you have to know how much money you will win if the market goes in your favor, and how much money you will lose if the market goes against you.

Don't never enter a trade in which the profit is less than the amount of money you risked.

If you will risk 100$ for example, your profit target should be at least 200$, this is a risk to reward ratio of 1:2.

Let's suppose that you took 10 trades with 1:2 risks to reward ratio. In every trade you risk 100$.

You won 5trades, and you lost 5 trades. So you will lose 500$.but you will win 1000$.so the benefits is 500$.

This is the power of the risk to reward ratio, you shouldn't think that you have to win all your trades to become a successful trader. If you can take the advantage of the risk to reward ratio, you will always be profitable.

The importance of a Stop loss

All good methodologies use stops. A protective stop loss is an order to exit a long or short position when prices move against you to specified price.

The stop loss insures against a usually large loss and has to be used in one way or another.

An initial stop loss can be placed with your order on the trading platform; the trade will be closed, automatically when if the stop loss is hit.

This type of stop loss will allow you to execute your trade and go spend time with your family or friends, this will help you to trade out of your emotion, because you know how much money you will lose if the market didn't go in your direction.

Lot of traders use mental stops, when they enter a trade, they don't place a stop loss, because they think that the broker will hit their stop loss which is not true.

The reason behind using mental stop is the human psychology, humans hate to lose money. And if you don't accept losing money as a part of the game, you will never make money in the market.

Don't never think of using mental stops, because you can't control the market, you can't be sure that the market will do this or that.

Before you enter a trade, calculate how much you may win, and how much you may lose. Place your stop loss order. And your profit target. And forget about your trade.

Don't ever risk money that you can't afford to lose

I got lot of questions from traders asking me about how much money they need to start trading. First of all, you have to take trading as a business. You can make money in this business and you can lose it as well.

THE CANDLESTICK TRADING BIBLE

The amount of money that you need to start trading depends on the amount of money that you can afford to lose. Don't ever borrow money or risk big amounts of money that you can't afford to lose.

Because trading is all about emotions, if you trade and you are afraid to lose your trading account, you will fail in this business. Because you will be controlled by your emotion, and this will affect your trading decisions.

You will not be able to follow your trading strategy, and you will certainly fail.

The best thing to do is to start small, try to get as much experience as you can, and build slowly your trading account. This is how successful traders become successful.

Conclusion

Congratulations, if you have made it to this point, this is a sign that you are hungry enough to succeed in this business. i have provided you with the most powerful price action strategies that you can use for the rest of your life to make money trading financial markets.

Your success as a trader has nothing to do with your educational background; you can be a doctor, a lawyer, or a physician scientist.

If you don't follow the rules, you will end up blowing up your entire trading account.

Trading is like learning a new skill, you must be ready to put in time and effort, let me give you an example, if you want to get a degree from a university, and you have to spend at least 3 years.

You wake up every morning, you study hard, you follow up with your classes, and if you are enough serious and disciplined, you get your degree.

The same thing when it comes to trading, if you are enough disciplined and you put in time and effort to learn, you will acquire a skill to feed yourself and your family for the rest of your life, you will get your financial freedom. So, you will never think of a day job.

Some traders spend more than 10 years to find a winning strategy and become profitable, others spend 20 years without results.

Fortunately, this will not be the case with you. Because you have the map, you have the strategy; you will not spend years trying different indicators and strategies.

You have everything you need here, what you will need is time to master these strategies, So give yourself some time and spend as much as can you to learn, because this is the only way to succeed in this business.

Over time you will develop these trading strategies, because you will determine what works for you, and what it doesn't work. Keep practicing, and learning from your mistakes, don't think in term of making money as fast as possible, think in term of becoming an expert of what you do, and then money will follow you wherever you are.

Good luck.

Made in the USA
Columbia, SC
25 February 2022